They went out to get the kind of result which would take us to Spain and they succeeded. Maybe we had a break or two, but in a cup competition any team needs that if it is going to be successful. We didn't get any more than our share.

One of the breaks came in that very first game we played in Stockholm. A great shot from one of their players hit the woodwork and bounced back onto Alan Rough, and big Alex McLeish stepped in to boot it away. To balance that, though, we might have had a couple of penalties. There was one glaring offence when Andy Gray was barged down in the box as he was getting ready for a header. Still, these things happen in any game and when Gordon Strachan went through to get that great goal in the second half it was enough for a win . . .

KENNY DALGLISH
WITH KEN GALLACHER

King Kenny

An Autobiography

PANTHER
Granada Publishing

Panther Books
Granada Publishing Ltd
8 Grafton Street, London W1X 3LA

This revised edition published by Panther Books 1984

First published in Great Britain by
Stanley Paul & Co. Ltd (Hutchinson Publishing Group) 1982

Copyright © Superstars Ltd and Ken Gallacher 1982, 1984

ISBN 0-586-06394-3

Printed and bound in Great Britain by
Collins, Glasgow

Set in Times

Contents

Acknowledgement

The author and publisher would like to thank the following for allowing the use of copyright photographs: Colorsport, Harry Ormesher, Press Association, Sportapics, Sporting Pictures (UK) Ltd, Syndication International

Introduction

In more than a decade at the top of his profession, Kenny Dalglish has played for just five managers. But that group includes some of the most successful and controversial team bosses in the game. Here they tell Ken Gallacher exactly what it is that has made Dalglish one of Scotland's greatest ever players.

Liverpool manager Bob Paisley, the man who bought Dalglish for £400,000 from Celtic and helped mould him into the man who made the Kop forget Kevin Keegan had this to say:

I suppose above everything else when you try to assess Kenny's importance you must talk about his attitude to the game. He just wants to play football.

Then, of course, he has tremendous skill and the ability to set the pace of the game for the other players around him. In that sense he is a remarkably influential player and that's something that the public don't always realize. In the game though, we can see this and it has been a vital part of our success. When I had to sell Kevin Keegan to Hamburg – and we didn't have any choice because Kevin wanted to go to Europe – I didn't think it would be possible to replace him. Yet we did it so easily just by buying Kenny from Celtic. I didn't have doubts about Kenny's ability at all, but I did think that he might take time to settle. That has happened before with players who move south from Scotland. But he came straight into the team in the Charity Shield game at Wembley and looked as if he had been a part of our setup all his life.

In many ways he has been a better player for Liverpool than Kevin was. The two of them have different qualities but as a team player I think Kenny is the more committed. He is a great professional and when he came into the team some of our players, people who had played with Kevin, were beginning to get that little bit older. They needed a player who could slow the pace of the game down and Kenny did that instinctively. He is a strong player too, and a marvellous passer of the ball.

He has played for us in the hardest position of all. Up front. On his own. Taking all the knocks that are handed out. Yet he never retaliates, just gets on with the game. He takes some whackings from defenders and yet he had that wonderful record for us of not missing a game in something like three seasons. That's a miracle, playing in the position he plays in. He is the target for all the hitmen in the game, especially on the Continent now when we play there. He is the man they are after – but few of them can kick him out of the game. Actually, when Kenny complains of a knock that's when you get worried, because you know it has to be a bad one before you'd hear any moans at all from him.

He's no prima donna either. With all the praise he has had, all the honours he has won, you might expect him to be, but he's the opposite – a model professional. He is the best buy we have ever made. It's as simple as that.

One time Manchester United Manager Tommy Docherty was the first Scotland manager to pick Kenny Dalglish. He started him on the run which has made the Liverpool star Scotland's most capped player. He says simply:

I consider myself lucky that I was the one who had the chance to give him his first cap for Scotland. Quite honestly there was no way that I could ignore him. He forced his way into that team and it's significant that he has never been out of the Scotland plans since. That's not surprising.

He has a terrible habit doesn't he – he just keeps getting goals. OK, like all strikers he has had lean spells. But you would never find Bob Paisley leaving him out, because even if he isn't getting goals regularly, you'll find that he is still playing well. That's the great thing about Kenny. He doesn't let his head go down simply because he might be having a difficult time. He'll keep on playing and working away as hard as he knows how. That's the way he sees the game. He sometimes gets criticized, particularly when playing for Scotland, but three other managers besides me have picked him because I think all of us have known his value. He isn't a flash player. He isn't someone who grabs the glory for himself. He submerges himself for the team effort.

When I take a look at Kenny Dalglish I feel that he is exactly the kind of player I'd want any youngster to model himself on. I suppose it must hurt him at times when he is criticized, but ask any of the players who work alongside him about his skills and you will learn just how his fellow professionals view his contributions. They may not always be obvious to the fans or the critics, but they are there, and what he has done in the game says more than anything else.

I had just one fall-out with him and again it tells you something about Kenny's attitude. I left him out of an Under-23 match once. He was just coming onto the international scene and I had him on the bench as a reserve. He didn't like that. Not because he was worried from an egotistical point of view. No, it was simply that he wasn't going to be playing. He lives for playing the game. That's all he wants to do. And he plays the game as well as any player I've known. And with the clubs I've handled, there's been a few of them.

Former Scotland Manager Willie Ormond, who died recently, left the national job to manage Hearts and then Hibs before quitting the game through ill health, capped Dalglish more than any other team boss. Looking back he said:

I consider Kenny Dalglish to be one of the greatest players ever to kick a ball. It always annoyed me when I was manager of Scotland – and it still annoys me now when I'm out of the game – to hear people criticizing him. All that nonsense about Kenny not playing well for his country. Not once did I think he let me down.

He thought he did in the World Cup finals in 1974, but I didn't think that. When we went to West Germany it was a new adventure for every one of these players. No one had been to the finals before and there we were in against Brazil and Yugoslavia, both very, very difficult teams to face. I thought that we were a little unlucky not to qualify and there was no way I felt disappointed by anyone's performances.

An awful lot of people simply don't appreciate what Kenny does on the field. My answer to the people who do criticize is, try to watch him when one of his team-mates has the ball! Don't just look at the ball all the time, take a look at the runs Kenny makes. Take a look at the spaces he finds. Watch how he always makes himself available for a pass. These things are of immense value to any team – the lads who play alongside him will tell you that.

Besides that, he has the ability to see situations quickly. I watched the 1981 World Club championship game against Flamengo on television. Liverpool were well beaten but Kenny set up one chance in the second half with what seemed the simplest of passes, which put Terry McDermott through. Kenny pushed it into that gap perfectly. And don't forget the goals he scores – a lot of important goals for Scotland.

There was never any doubt in my mind when he was transferred that he would be a success with Liverpool. I know that other players have not hit it off down south, but Kenny was a natural to fit in straightaway. He has the talent, and he also has the right attitude to the game. In almost forty internationals and a few Under-23 games as well, I can't remember one moment's trouble from Kenny. If you were looking for an example for a young player to follow then he would be the player I'd pick out.

I'm sure he'll be a key figure in Spain because he has the experience needed to play at that level. He has gained it in two previous finals, and you can't do well at that level with a team of youngsters. Over the years I've been in the game, I've seen and played with a lot of good players and I'd put Kenny in the elite group of Scots that would also include Bobby Johnstone and Torry Gillick.

As for the record-breaking consecutive number of caps,* I honestly cannot remember the occasion, though obviously it would mean a lot to Kenny. But I do know this, I'd only leave a player out if I felt there was perhaps someone else going to do the job better. It wouldn't be in my mind that records could be broken or anything like that. All I concerned myself with was picking the right men for the right job. But I'm glad that Kenny has beaten that record now, because I can't think of anyone who deserves to hold it more than he does. He has earned anything he gets out of the game, because he has put more into it than most.

* See page 61

Ally MacLeod was the third Scotland boss to pick Kenny Dalglish and it was in Ally's reign that Kenny passed Denis Law's record number of caps for his country. Now out of football and running a successful pub in Kilmarnock, Ally had this to say:

Kenny is a manager's dream player. No trouble. Never a complaint. He'll go out and do a job for you no matter what it is you ask from him. You can go on all day about his skills. He turns defenders as well as the best of the Continental forwards and he is as strong as any player you can name. You've just got to watch him being tackled from the back to know that.

Sometimes I've felt that he hasn't always been played in his best position for Scotland. I blame myself for that as much as anyone else. He has been played off someone like Joe Jordan or Andy Gray when at Liverpool they play off him. I tried it that way twice. When we played friendly games in Chile and in Argentina before the 1978 World Cup finals, I used Kenny as the target-man up front with little Lou Macari playing off him. It worked in both games, and I'm only sorry that I didn't persist. I thought of doing it against Iran, for instance, and then changed my mind. It might have made all the difference.

It annoys me to hear people argue about how Kenny plays for Scotland and the suggestion that he never does well.

People in the pub tend to say that he does more for Liverpool than he does for Scotland. Maybe there is a grain of truth in that – but no more than that. In my time as manager I can remember some quite outstanding performances from him. There were two of the vital qualifying games, against Czechoslovakia at Hampden and then against Wales at Anfield. He scored in each of these and was superb. Then against Holland in our final game in Argentina he was magnificent and he scored there too. There are plenty of other examples – England at Wembley, for instance when we beat them when I was manager.

I think that he has been sadly underrated by some of the Scots fans. It makes me laugh to hear them in the pub talking about the great performances of Denis Law or Jim Baxter. They forget that these two players got a lot of stick too when they had bad games for Scotland. But that was ten or fifteen years ago and the good games are remembered, the others forgotten. In ten years' time people will be looking back at Kenny's career and then he will be one of our football heroes. Rightly so. He is one of the finest players ever to wear a Scotland jersey. He will be a legend in years to come, mark my words.

One more thing – there is not a better, more dedicated professional in the game.

Scotland manager Jock Stein, Kenny's first boss when he began his career with Celtic, had this to say about Dalglish:

I don't think you could have a better player to handle than Kenny Dalglish. His strength has always been his enthusiasm for the game. For Celtic and Liverpool he has given his best all the time. He is exactly the type of player you always want in you side.

He wants to play all the time, sometimes when he shouldn't. He has played when he is unfit when his club needed him. As a Celtic player he gave the club 100 per cent all the time.

He has proved all there is to prove about his ability by moving on to Liverpool to take over from Kevin Keegan. Liverpool bought a player – and sold a player. I think they bought a better player than Keegan. I think they bought a better club man than Keegan. And they made a profit on the deal.

When he goes onto the field Kenny leaves all his problems behind him. All he wants is to get out there and play football. His attitude cannot be bettered. He has his critics. What good player doesn't? But I cannot see that anyone can criticize him from a purely football point of view. They might dislike some things about him, but his ability and his approach cannot be questioned.

I just feel that there's a block which means that he doesn't play as consistently well for Scotland as he does for his club. That can be for many reasons. The setup may be different. It may be harder for him to adjust or to change his style. But it still doesn't make any difference to his approach. He still gives you 100 per cent.

He has been an astonishing player for Liverpool. They have used him in the hardest position of all: up front as their main striker. There have been times recently when he has looked as if he has been too long in the firing line and I can understand that and accept it. When he had an indifferent spell as a striker with Celtic we used to drop him back into the midfield for a spell until the sharpness returned; and Liverpool have been doing that too. He'll play as well for them there. Anyone who writes off Kenny Dalglish is wrong. Some people say that he is nearing the end. I don't see that. Kenny Dalglish will be about for a wee while yet. No matter where Liverpool play him or where I play him for Scotland, we'll be sure, Bob Paisley and I, that we will get everything he has to offer. He doesn't know any other way to play. There's an honesty about his play that an awful lot of players could learn from.

1
Transferred at midnight!

It was like a scene from one of those spy films, the scene where an exchange is taking place at a deserted border post . . .

Yet all that was happening was a footballer, me, being transferred from one club to another. I'll never forget that August night in 1977 that took me from Celtic to Liverpool, nor how the Celtic ground looked as I drove up to it at approaching midnight. The car park in front of the main stand was deserted except for a huddle of two or three darkened cars right outside the main entrance – and just two lights glowed, one in manager Jock Stein's office and the other in the boardroom.

At this time all I knew was that I had been summoned to the ground by the Boss after a day of rumours about my future. And ten minutes or so earlier he had told me on the phone that Liverpool were interested in me and could I come to the ground.

Within minutes of meeting the Liverpool chairman Mr John Smith and manager Bob Paisley I had agreed to sign for them – and the rumours were over!

It was the end of a summer of discontent for me. Not the first one I had had at Celtic Park, but the most critical, because it did end with me leaving the club I had joined as a teenager so many years before.

The break hadn't arrived suddenly, because the problems between myself and Celtic had been simmering for several months. I say 'problems' because there was never any trouble between myself and the club. It was just that I thought my future lay elsewhere. I wanted somehow to prove myself and my ability in the English First Division.

Anyhow, it was before the end of the previous season that I had first told manager Jock Stein that I wanted to go. I had refused to sign the new contract he offered me and when he attempted to talk me round, I dug in my heels. I'm sure, looking back, that he thought I would change my mind just as I had done a year earlier when I had asked the club for a transfer.

Then I had talked it over with my wife Marina who was expecting our first baby in September, but I don't think I had gone into all the details sufficiently. Plus I had asked when the Boss was away in hospital recovering from a car crash. His assistant manager Sean Fallon was running things, the club captain Billy McNeill had retired only a year before, and when I began to feel pressure on me to stay I changed my mind. I felt that I was letting the club down at a time when it perhaps needed me most.

I remember saying to Sean Fallon at the time, 'I'm sorry to be adding to your worries. I know you have a lot of them now that the Boss is in hospital and I don't like making them worse . . .'

It was because of all that, I think, that I withdrew the request and decided that I would stay with the club. Celtic had been good to me and I couldn't just leave them in the lurch. So I signed a contract which I honoured. The unhappiness remained, though, and when at the end of the first year the contract was up and I was offered a new one to sign, I refused. I told the Boss that I wasn't going to be persuaded this time!

Eventually though I did agree to sign, but stressed that I still wanted to leave Celtic. The only reason I had for putting my name to a new contract was to help the club. We were scheduled to play Rangers in a Scottish Cup final and if I had not been registered with a new contract then it could have leaked out to the press that I hadn't signed. As I was Celtic captain it would have looked bad . . . and it would have added to the pressures on the lads which always built up in any case before an Old Firm final. Players must be registered with the Scottish Football Association by a certain date. If I hadn't signed and was playing on my option, it would soon have been known outside the club. That was the one and only reason I did sign, because I still wanted a transfer and this time I was not going to change my mind!

After the 1977 Cup Final – we won it 1–0 and I collected my fourth winner's medal – I left with the Scotland team for the home internationals and then a tour of South America. But before going I had a meeting with Mr Stein to insist that I wanted a transfer. I did not want him thinking that I was going to be influenced by stories from other players in the Scotland squad. I stated my reasons for signing and reiterated that I wanted to leave. We had games to play in Chile, Argentina and Brazil . . . all intended as warm-up games if we qualified for the World Cup finals the following summer in Argentina. (Of these finals, more later . . .)

It was a good summer, that one. We drew with Wales in Wrexham, beat Northern Ireland at Hampden 3–0, beat England at Wembley 2–0 and went to South America for the tour as British champions. Even there we did fine. We won our opening match in Santiago against Chile 4–2, drew 1–1 with Argentina in Buenos Aires and our only defeat came in the Maracana stadium in Rio where Brazil beat us 2–0.

I came home feeling good, but knowing too that my future had still to be resolved. By now I was absolutely determined that my future was in England and I had even talked things over with one of the more experienced Anglos in the Scotland squad. And I'd like to make it clear right now that I approached *him* about it. Things didn't happen the other way round. It's always being said that Anglos, Scottish players based with clubs in England, are forever luring players south with talk of the big money to be earned there. No one ever came to me with these tales. Anyone who can read a newspaper has some idea of what the top men in England can pick up. You don't have to be approached!

But this time, knowing that I wasn't going to stay, knowing that I was not going to allow Celtic to persuade me to change my mind once more, I did look for advice. I was given the advice I wanted. No more than that. The player concerned didn't guide me towards any club . . . he simply told me of the various wage structures as far as he knew them and of the conditions at different places.

I had a short break at home as I didn't have time for a family holiday, and then reported back to Celtic Park. It was then that the rift between myself and the club became public – though neither myself nor Jock Stein had wanted it that way. Celtic were fixed for a tour of Australia and the Boss asked Danny McGrain and myself if we would go even though we had had a long, hard summer of playing and travelling. Danny agreed that he would make the trip. I didn't.

Privately I told the Boss my reasons: that I still wanted to leave and that he would be better planning for the new season without me as a part of the side. It wasn't an argument he was ready to listen to. He told me I was under contract. I told him that I had only signed that contract to prevent problems before the Cup Final. He told me that the tour organizers wanted me to be there. I told him that wasn't my problem. So it went on . . . but

Jock Stein can be powerfully persuasive and before I left the ground I found myself agreeing to come in that afternoon with my boots and that I'd leave with the team the next morning. But he must have realized that I was determined to leave Celtic because he told me he would telephone a club who could be interested in buying me.

I went home that lunchtime, sat down and talked things out with Marina once more. There was no way I could see any future in going to Australia. Not for me nor for the club. So that afternoon I drove back to Celtic Park minus my boots. Neilly Mochan the coach was waiting for me to bring them in to be packed in the hamper. I told him that I wasn't going, and then I had to see the Boss again. I told him that I didn't even want to know the outcome of the phone call he had made because I was not going to Australia.

I was determined that he wouldn't talk me round this time. 'Look,' he told me, 'why don't you sleep on it and call me in the morning. If you've changed your mind come straight to the airport and we'll see to the other business (the transfer request) when we get back home!'

That was tempting. There was no way I wanted to leave the club under a cloud. I didn't relish the idea of everyone suddenly knowing that there was trouble over the tour or anything else. I agreed, but in the morning he phoned me and said, 'It's best for us to take players who want to play for the club.' I said OK and that was that. It was how I had felt all along anyway. I think that's when he knew that there was no way at all that he could ever talk me into staying at Celtic Park.

Off the team went and then the panic began as the newspapers realized that I wasn't in the party which flew out. They besieged the house, but I didn't say anything. It was up to the club to handle things from that time on. I'd told them what I wanted and I knew that they would know that this time I really did mean business. Nothing would change my mind.

While the first team were on tour I trained with the reserves at Parkhead. I did that quite happily because I felt that I didn't want to leave the club with any more bad feeling than could be helped. Obviously I knew that they weren't going to be pleased to lose me but I didn't want to give any other causes for complaint. It wasn't the way I wanted to treat Celtic after playing just over 200 first-team matches for them.

When the tour ended, the Boss asked me once more if I had changed my mind. I stood my ground. 'Nothing's changed,' I told him. 'I still want to leave the club.'

On the Friday there was a game at Stirling against Stirling Albion and I played in it with the reserve-team lads. Brian McLaughlin, who is now with Motherwell, was skipper of the reserves and I was club captain. Naturally I thought I would take the team out but he was given that honour. Maybe Brian was embarrassed but I wasn't because I knew that something had to happen soon. The following Tuesday, 10 August, there was another warm-up match. This one was at Dunfermline and was a first-team game. I was in the side, but just before the kickoff the Boss handed the ball to Danny McGrain and told him, 'Take them out.' He was right to do that in my opinion. He knew and I knew that my time with Celtic was over and his job was to look to the future, and that future had my mate Danny as the new club captain. So my career with Celtic, begun as a teenager, ended that night at Dunfermline where only a few thousand people watched us win 4–1, where I lost the captaincy, and where few people at the game realized that it was my final match for the club.

In fact, I didn't realize it myself. I was still wondering if I would be playing against Dundee United in the opening League game the following Saturday as Mr Stein was quoted as saying in the newspapers! Sure there were rumours – they had been buzzing around Glasgow all day. And there were some more substantial hints – but they came after the match!

When I came out of the visitors' dressing room there was a throng of pressmen waiting to see me. I could tell them nothing – because I simply didn't know anything. But two of them, Ken Gallacher of the *Daily Record* and Jim Rodger of the *Daily Mirror*, told me that the word was out that Liverpool manager Bob Paisley had driven north with his chairman and had been sitting in the East End Park stand.

I had a cup of tea with the other players and then we left on the team bus for Glasgow and Celtic Park. Still no one from the club said anything at all to me, though one of the other players, Alfie Conn, said he had heard the Liverpool stories as well. Meanwhile the Boss had left Dunfermline with our club chairman, Mr Desmond White, and didn't come with the players on the team bus as usual. When we got back to Celtic Park there was still silence and I put the press interest down to rumours and speculation once again. I left the ground with goalkeeper Peter Latchford and drove over to the pub my father-in-law runs in Rutherglen. Peter relaxed with a pint while I had my usual soft drink, and we sat and blethered; he was asking me if I thought I would be on the move soon when the phone rang and I was told that Marina was calling me.

When I answered she said simply, 'The Boss has been on the phone for you here at the house. You have to call him at Celtic Park straightaway!'

My mind was ticking over now as I made that call.

Surely, I thought, something has happened. Maybe someone has come in for me and they'll want to see me tomorrow.

The so familiar voice of the Boss answered and he asked me first of all, 'Have you changed your mind about leaving?' When I told him no, he said, 'Well, Liverpool are here and they want to speak to you. They would like to see you now . . . unless you have changed your mind.'

He told me not to tell anyone and to drive straight to the ground. That's what I did. The Boss asked me again if I'd changed my mind and when I told him I hadn't, he let me speak to Liverpool. He took me through to the boardroom and that's when I met Bob Paisley and Mr Smith for the first time. They told me that the two clubs had agreed on a fee – something I'd realized from the fact that I was being allowed to speak to them – and they told me the approximate terms they would offer me if I was willing to sign. I didn't mess about. Inside a few minutes I had agreed to join Liverpool and Mr Paisley and Mr Smith asked me if I could travel down to Moffat to meet them at their hotel the next morning. From there we would head on to Anfield, where a press conference was to be arranged for the signing. It was hard to believe that the months of agonizing had been settled so quickly in the end. All along, deep down, Liverpool were the club I had wanted to go to. Their record had appealed to me and the stories I'd heard about the family atmosphere at Anfield sounded good too. I drove home in a daze.

I told Marina the terms which had been explained to me by Mr Paisley and Mr Smith. Money was not the most important thing about the move but it affects everyone's thinking when it comes to their careers and I'm no different from anyone else as far as that goes. But it wasn't the be-all and end-all. If I had remained with Celtic then I

would have had a testimonial match – the club had told me
as much – just the same as other players had had before
me, and as Danny McGrain was to do after me. But that
kind of massive payoff wasn't what I needed at that stage
of my career. I wanted fresh challenges. I still had
ambition – and it hasn't left me yet – and I knew that I
wanted to win as many top awards in the game as possible.
Over the years with Celtic I'd taken everything I could in
the Scottish game but the furthest we had gone in Europe
was the semifinal of the European Cup, when Atletico
Madrid booted us off the field in the most troubled game
I've ever played in. Really I wanted to taste success in
Europe . . . and that kind of ambition had been bred into
me in my early days at Celtic Park.

At Celtic Park we were reared on success – and we got
that success. In my seven seasons with the first team –
that's from my debut mind you – I played 200 league
games and won five championship medals. Add to that
four Scottish Cup winner's badges and a League Cup
winner's medal and you'll see I had my share of success at
Parkhead.

But – and it was a big but – when I grew up there as a
young player I was mixing with the Lisbon Lions – the first
players to bring the European Cup to Britain. Bobby
Murdoch and Billy McNeill and Jimmy Johnstone and
Bertie Auld and the rest were at the Park when I started
off. The team reached another European Cup final after
that 1967 win – when they lost to Feyenoord in Milan in
1970. After that Celtic breakthrough, other British clubs
moved in and eventually came to dominate the tournament. That was in my mind when I wanted to move on and
it was also in my mind that Liverpool – already winners in
that marvellous final in Rome – would be well equipped to
do it all over again. That's the kind of success I was

searching for. And I did want to prove myself in the English First Division which has been called the best League in Europe.

Money couldn't get me what I wanted – Liverpool could. And over the years, they have provided me with everything that I could have asked for from the game. That's what made it the right move for me. Not the kind of money I could make in the south, but the fulfilment of the ambitions which had been sown in my mind as a youngster at Celtic Park. It was a very special atmosphere then. I was lucky to develop as a player with so many good men around me ready to guide me both on and off the field.

Liverpool had that same feel about it even in the whirlwind first few days I spent there. At midnight on the Tuesday I agreed to sign . . . and the following afternoon at a ballyhooed press conference I did sign . . . and three days later I was playing in the Charity Shield game at Wembley against Manchester United in front of a sell-out crowd. We drew 0–0 incidentally, and the Liverpool fans were marvellous to me. It was hectic. It was glamorous. It was challenging. It was all that I'd dreamed about . . .

On the previous Thursday, of course, I had been brought down to earth with my first Anfield training session. It was as hard as any training session I'd ever known, and it emphasized to me the high standards of the club I had joined. I remember thinking about that when I got back to the hotel where I was staying. Until then I hadn't had the time to think. That day though, I knew that Liverpool was where I belonged.

Before the game at Wembley, my old Celtic mate Lou Macari had said in the tunnel on the way out to the field, 'Why didn't you tell me you wanted away? My club might have been interested, we might have come for you.'

Teaming up with Lou again and all the marvellous

tradition of Old Trafford, that was quite a thought going
up that Wembley tunnel. I hadn't told Lou that I wanted a
move. I'd only asked one player in the Scotland squad for
guidance and he had respected my trust. I'm respecting his
now, because I'm not going to name him, even though
there was no way that he influenced my decision. He
simply gave me good advice. No one else on that close-
season tour had had a hint that I would be away from
Celtic the following season.

But no matter who had come in, I'm sure that Liverpool
would have been my choice above any other club. I don't
think anything has proved that choice wrong.

2

Invited to join Celtic – and worried how to tell my dad!

The Lisbon Lions were still ruling Scottish soccer and the memory of their Lisbon triumph over Inter Milan hadn't faded from anyone's memory. Yet when I was asked to train at Celtic Park for the first time, I had reservations. The kind which could only come from being born and having grown up in a city with divided soccer loyalties.

My loyalties as a schoolboy had been with Rangers. They were the team I went to see, the team I supported, and I can still reel off the names of the side I saw most of: Ritchie, Shearer, Caldow, Davis, Paterson, Baxter, Scott, McMillan, Millar, Brand, Wilson.

It was a very good team, too. Before I started playing football on a Saturday afternoon, my father took me all over Scotland to watch Rangers. I don't think that I ever consciously copied anyone but, when I was old enough to concentrate and to pay attention properly, Ian McMillan and Jim Baxter were my favourites. McMillan, who spent most of his years with Airdrie before joining Rangers, was what would be called now an old-fashioned Scottish inside forward. He was a very skilled player and, of course, so was Baxter. Baxter was perhaps more flamboyant. But, while my father insists that there are times when he can see touches of McMillan in my play, I never tried to play like him or anyone else.

At that time Celtic didn't enter my thinking. I was a Rangers' supporter and these loyalties had been nourished by my father who had always supported the

Ibrox club, the other half of Scotland's Old Firm – and Celtic's greatest rivals. So you can understand how I felt when Bob Keir who ran the Glasgow United side I played with told me, 'Celtic would like you to go up to Parkhead for training.'

On one hand I was being asked to join the players who had become the best team in Scotland . . . on the other they were the rivals of the team I had always supported. Quite honestly, I just didn't know what to say to my dad. After all, he'd started taking me to Ibrox when I was only about five years old.

Now here I was asked to train with Celtic – I went home that night and didn't even tell my dad about the chance I had been given. The next morning I left the house still without telling him; then, later that night, Bob Keir let dad know and he talked to me about it. He was great actually. Obviously he would have preferred it if I had been signing for Rangers – but he also realized that I was going to the club that was the best in Scotland and the club where I would probably get the very best soccer education.

Anyhow, quite simply, Rangers hadn't come for me. Their chief scout at that time, a former centre forward with the club, Jimmy Smith, kept telling people that I was going to finish up at Ibrox. And these same people kept telling my dad the same thing. But no one from Ibrox ever came to the door, even though I didn't live so very far from the ground. By that time we had moved to the multi-storey flats near Ibrox. In fact, my bedroom window looked down on the Rangers training ground at the Albion. That's how close I was to the team I supported.

After I had decided to train at Celtic Park – with my dad's blessing – Sean Fallon, the assistant manager, arrived at the house one night to see my parents. That was a panic!

While my mum was going to answer the door I was

rushing about getting the Rangers pictures off the wall in the living room. I know that story went about Glasgow as a kind of joke – but it was true. And on the night, it was no joke. Luckily, Sean saw the funny side. He had to, I suppose, because I hadn't managed to get all the pictures down.

People always ask me who my favourite Rangers player was when I was a kid and I honestly can't remember, but my dad tells me that my first hero was Don Kichenbrand. He was a South African centre forward, the Rhino, they nicknamed him, and from what I've been told he was a big, burly, old-fashioned battering ram of a player. Yet my dad insists that when I first began going to the games at Ibrox, Kichenbrand was my idol. My father tells me that when Rangers eventually transferred Kichenbrand to Sunderland I was in tears when I heard the news. Sammy Baird was another player I liked then and I used to go into the barber's shop and ask him to cut my hair like Big Sammy's. Things change . . .

Although I was playing with Glasgow United when Celtic spotted me, I had started off with Possil YM because I was then staying in the Milton area of Glasgow. I was actually born, on 4 March 1951, over in Dalmarnock, on the other side of Glasgow, not too far from Celtic Park. But the family moved to Milton when I was just ten months old. After that, we made another move to the flat near Rangers' ground.

According to the family I started kicking a ball about on the waste ground in that Milton housing scheme when I was about five years old. Funnily enough one of the neighbours then was Ian Ross who went on to play for Liverpool and Aston Villa and is now a coach with Wolves. He was about three years older than me.

Another neighbour was George Andrews who went to West Ham. He was the same age as Ian.

Anyhow we had a team, just a street team, called Milton Milan. We wore the all-white Inter Milan strip and we thought we were the greatest thing ever. It was the way most boys in Glasgow started playing the game but we thought we were a cut above the others because instead of jackets for goal posts we had special collapsible ones, made for us by the father of one of the team.

A few years later, when I was about eight or nine, I began to get a game for the school but as a goalkeeper. It was a case of playing in any position to get a game. After a while they let me play outfield. I'm glad now because I don't think I'd ever have rivalled big Clem!

When I was coming up for twelve I transferred companies in the Boys' Brigade. The company I was in, connected with my parents' church, didn't have a football team, so I moved to another outfit. It meant that I could play for the school in the morning and then with the BB team in the afternoon. It was when I was playing with the BB side that Possil YM approached me and I was offered the chance of joining them.

Quite a few players came from Possil – Eddie Kelly who was with Arsenal, Johnny Hamilton who was with Hibs and Rangers, and Robert Russell of Rangers. It was a good breeding ground for players.

I moved on to Glasgow United and I was with their Under-16 team when Vic Davidson – who joined Celtic with me – and Fred Pethard of Torquay United were there. I think we had the best team for that age group in Scotland. We were asked to play a game at Celtic's training ground under lights, against their provisional signings. Paul Wilson, another of my Celtic team-mates in later years, was playing against us. At the end of the

match we had won 3–2 and it was then that I was asked to
go back and train. Not too long after that I was given the
chance to sign.

Of course, before that, I'd kept up my school team
activities and after the seemingly endless series of trials I
was picked twice to play for the Scotland Schoolboys'
Under-15s team. We met England at Ibrox where we drew
1–1 and before that we went to Belfast and beat the Irish
boys 4–3. Tommy Craig was one of my team-mates and he
went on to play for Aberdeen and then several English
clubs. It's really amazing how people I played with at
school or in the Boys' Brigade or even in the street, keep
cropping up again in later years. Paths seem to be crossing
all the time.

By this time my dad was encouraging me all the way.
He told me just to concentrate on the playing side and
forget everything else. He didn't want me being worried
by any Celtic–Rangers problems. Not that there were any
serious problems, but I had to take a bit of kidding from
my mates because they knew how keen I had been about
Rangers, especially when I was younger. There was
always going to be some kind of comeback wasn't there?
But I was able to handle it – with a little help from my dad.
He emphasized to me that all that mattered was helping
my career and if Celtic were going to do that, then that
was the club to sign for.

Celtic wanted me to play with a junior team for
experience and they arranged all that. The Celtic scout
Frank Meechan took me out to see Cumbernauld United
and that's the club I joined as a junior player. I played for
them against Glasgow Perthshire and we won 3–0, then I
was in against Yoker Athletic and we won 5–1 and after
that they asked me to sign. Of course, they got me for
nothing because I was a provisional signing with Celtic. I

signed the forms for them at half time during a game at Neilston against the local junior team. Meanwhile I was serving my apprenticeship as a joiner. Celtic wanted me to gain experience and I did that in my spell with the juniors. I was given a good grounding, and while I was playing and training with my Cumbernauld team-mates I was also continuing to train at Celtic Park usually one night a week.

Gradually, I realized that football had to be my full-time career. The joinery apprenticeship was not doing too much for me any more, and so I began seriously to consider trying to make football my life. After training one night I went in to see Jock Stein and ask him if I could go full-time with the club. That's what I wanted, I told him. Naturally he knew I had a good job and he didn't want to rush me. He suggested that maybe I should play another year as a junior before he called me up. I didn't want that. I wanted to chuck my job and get to Celtic Park right away.

Luckily, once again my dad stepped in. He knew what I wanted most and he agreed with me, so he went in to speak to Jock Stein about it all.

He convinced the Boss that it was in my interests to let me have a go at full-time football. That was it – I was called up from the juniors and went straight into the reserve team. Now the real learning started . . .

Celtic was a marvellous place to be as a young player. There were so many good players around you and all of them willing to pass on tips that might help. There was nothing clannish about the place. People who remember me as a young player have told me that I was a ringer for Bobby Murdoch at that time. I wasn't conscious of that. I did play midfield then and people did compare us, but there was no way that I tried to ape his style. Certainly I wasn't aware of doing it. It may just have been the continuity in the coaching at the club then. Bobby as a young player had been coached by Jock Stein when he was in charge of the reserves at Celtic Park. Now I was there being coached by Big Jock and Willie Fernie. Maybe it was some of the traditional coaching values in the club that rubbed off on me and, for that spell, brought Bobby into people's minds when they watched me. At any rate I don't remember being allowed to pick up any bad habits in that period. It was pretty inspiring just to be around all these players who seemed, then, to have travelled most of the football world and learned something everywhere they had been. The longer I mixed with them, the more my dad's words came back to me – that I was going to the club where I would get the best kind of football education.

My mate at the start – and my mate still today – was Danny McGrain. I started training in the same close season as he did. We were around the same age, had been training in midweek together, and now we went into the reserves at the same time. It was a good reserve team, too. There were experienced players around in that side. Joe McBride was the centre forward, Davie Cattanach was in the side and Jim Brogan was in and out of the team as well. It's hard looking back at all the games but I do remember qualifying from a Reserve League Cup section which included ourselves, Rangers and Partick Thistle. This entailed playing in my first Old Firm game at Ibrox. I was only seventeen years old and Rangers had in their second team Alex Smith and Dave Smith, two experienced players bought from Dunfirmline and Aberdeen respectively for around £100,000 – a lot of money in those days. I felt a bit overawed going in against them, yet we won the match 1–0. Despite that we still had to beat Partick Thistle by 7–0 to win the section and qualify for a place in the knockout stages of the tournament. We went berserk and won 12–0! That took us through instead of Rangers and I remember one of their youngest players – he's still at Ibrox – defender Alex Miller, saying that they got the paper, saw the score and thought it was a misprint. They couldn't believe it. Nor could I. It was already a long way from Cumbernauld United.

As well as the experienced players, we had Danny McGrain, John Gorman, who later went to Spurs and is now in the States, Davie Hay and George Connelly in that reserve team. Later on a few of us used to hang about together and were called 'the Quality Street Gang'. The gang comprised myself, Victor Davidson, Davie Hay, George Connelly, Lou Macari, Paul Wilson and Danny McGrain – all the lads who eventually broke through into the first team. And all of us, except Vic and Paul, went on to play for Scotland.

I suppose the biggest regret of all of us from that group is that George Connelly gave up the game when he did and in the way he did. It was a tragedy. Big Geordie had everything going for him. He was what the coaches call the 'modern defender'. I remember him playing against West Germany at Hampden one night and looking as much the perfect sweeper as Franz Beckenbauer. Then he threw it all away. He just upped and left the game when everything was there in front of him. He would have been in the World Cup squad in West Germany in 1974. He could have been in the squad still today.

It's hard to say what made George walk out on Celtic. He had done it before – he walked out of Glasgow Airport one morning instead of coming with Scotland to Switzerland for an international match. He'd been forgiven for that one and then he left Celtic. Of course all of us talked about it – we wouldn't have been human if we hadn't talked about something like that – but while we all knew that George had been hard to get to know, very deep, and a player who kept himself to himself all the time, none of us came any closer to understanding what had happened.

George came from Fife and his whole family, his brothers and everyone else, were Celtic daft. So was George. He loved the Celtic. He really did. Which is why it is so difficult to figure out why he left the club. I don't think he liked living in the west of Scotland. He had moved down to Blantyre from his own home area and that didn't suit him. But there was no obvious reason why he should have done what he did . . .

I think that most footballers, probably something like 90 per cent of the professionals in this country, come from working-class backgrounds. So if you are successful, it can be difficult to get used to that kind of success. You don't get too much of a private life, temptations are put in your way, bright lights, call it what you will, and George was essentially a quiet lad. He didn't want people coming up to him in the street. He wanted a peaceful life and in football that isn't always possible.

The first time George left Celtic, Big Jock was able to bring him back and before he came to training the Boss asked all of us not to say too much to him. Clearly the Boss didn't want anyone to ask him what was going on or kid him at all. It would have made things worse. In a dressing room there is often a lot of stick flying about – whether you deserve it or not. You just have to learn to live with that. This time though, we all knew that it was something serious and we respected the Big Man and gave that respect to George as well.

Now though, I wonder if maybe we didn't try too hard to help him. All of us – especially the younger ones who had played with him since reserve-team days – wanted him to get things together and get back into the team. So we went out of our way to be helpful and maybe that was as bad as kidding him about things; maybe it made him feel just as self-conscious. I just don't know. We did all try but we failed and Scotland lost one of its great players.

When Scotland clinched qualification for the 1974 World Cup by beating Czechoslovakia at Hampden Park in September 1973, George was one of five Celtic players in the team – half the side, if you like! The others were Ally Hunter, Davie Hay, Danny McGrain and myself. The following Saturday we went to Perth, all of us played and we lost to St Johnstone! It's funny to look back now and see what has happened to the five. George and Ally are out of the game altogether; Davie Hay, after a series of injury blows following the finals of that World Cup in West Germany, is with Motherwell as manager; Danny and I are still in the Scotland squad.

Danny, of course, has remained with Celtic all those years while I elected to move on – something that the Celtic fans haven't let me forget!

That's the one thing which has saddened me since I left Scotland for Liverpool. I thought that I had the same relationship with the Celtic fans as I have with the Kop. I thought too that it would be long-lasting. Forever, if you like. Then I went back to play at Celtic Park for Liverpool and I was given a rude awakening. It was a pre-season testimonial match for Jock Stein on his retirement as Celtic manager. All the lads at Anfield were telling me how the fans would be waiting for me. 'It'll be like going home again, Kenny,' they said. How wrong can you be?

I got stick. From before the game started until the end I was the target for a lot of the Celtic fans. The only thing that saved me was that I knew what was going to happen. The talk was out among the supporters that they would

give me a roasting when I came back – and that's just
what they did. The grapevine at the pub in Rutherglen
picked it all up so I told the Liverpool lads before I went
onto the field, 'I'm going to get stick here tonight.' They
didn't believe me until we came out of that tunnel. Then
it hit them – and not a single one of them could understand it.

I did though. It didn't matter to the punters that I had
spent many years with the club. It didn't matter how many
times I'd played for Celtic or how many championships or
Scottish Cups I'd helped them win. It didn't matter how
many goals I'd scored for them. All that had been wiped
out when I said I wanted to leave. That's what they
couldn't understand. Those supporters who go there week
after week, often standing in the same place on the
terracing or in the 'Jungle', just couldn't accept that
anyone would want to leave their team.

If it had been someone they didn't want to see in the
team then that would have been fine. But I didn't come
into that category. As far as they were concerned I had
turned my back on the only team which mattered. I could
understand that because I'd known Celtic supporters for a
long, long time . . . But it still hurt. Even though I'd
known beforehand that something was going to happen, it
still hurt.

I'd tried not to provoke resentments. I had never said
anything against the club all through the transfer business.
Nor did I want to. I had never said anything against the
supporters either. Again, why should I have wanted to?
They had been great to me and I thought that good will
would continue right through my career. But, like I say,
they looked on me as a traitor because in their eyes I
turned my back on their club. I didn't see it that way.
From the time I joined the club as a sixteen-year-old

provisional signing, through my first team debut against
Raith Rovers in 1969 until the day I left to join Liverpool
in 1977, I had given them everything I had. Even now
Celtic's is the first score I want to hear when I'm in the
bath with the Liverpool lads after a game. That's not
going to change. Even the booing and jeering I got that
night won't alter my feelings for the club. Though I must
admit that that testimonial game was the first time since
I'd been sixteen years of age that I was happy to see a
Celtic team lose. At least I'd had some revenge against the
fans – though, honestly, I don't hold any grudges. I did
what I had to do at the time and they just didn't
understand.

That return apart, my Celtic memories are good ones
and I left the club with genuine regret. The bonus I had
was in going to the same kind of club, in Liverpool, and in
rejoining very quickly the same kind of atmosphere.

Both teams had the comradeship that is vital to success
and which cannot be bought. So I consider myself lucky
that my only two senior clubs have been the same in that
so vital sense.

I don't think I'll ever forget playing my first full game
for Celtic. Bobby Murdoch came up to me when I was
sitting in the dressing room and asked me if I was at all
nervous. Really I think he knew that I was, and with my
playing in his position he had come up to lift my confidence a little and get rid of any pre-match butterflies.
Still, I had to pretend that I was OK. 'I'm fine,' I told him.
'I feel great. No problems.'

'Then,' grinned Bobby, 'why don't you start trying to
put these boots on the right feet?'

It's for that kind of tension-relieving crack, that kind of
dressing-room friendship, that I'll remember Celtic.
When I do I'll be thankful that Sean Fallon didn't mind

too much about those Rangers pictures the night he came
to my house to sign me. Otherwise my career might have
taken a different turn – and it couldn't have been one for
the better.

3
Life with Liverpool

From the time I signed for Liverpool in 1977, the inevitable comparisons have been made between myself and Kevin Keegan. I say inevitable because it's always seemed to me obvious that the newspapers and TV would seek to link my arrival with Kevin's departure from Liverpool. Yet as far as I was concerned at the time, I wasn't being signed to take over Keegan's role in the Liverpool team. Nor do I think that Bob Paisley signed me to do that.

In fact, I *know* he didn't. For one very simple reason: he told me so!

The Boss underlined to me that he didn't look to me to take over Kevin's role. What he wanted from me was the form I had shown with Celtic and with Scotland. He stressed that he didn't want me to alter my style to try to be another Kevin. The only similarity was that I took over the number seven shirt which had been his during his time with the club. You know, I don't think even the fans expected a carbon-copy replacement. I honestly believe that no one could have copied Kevin when he went to Hamburg. They didn't want someone who would try to emulate Kevin Keegan and fail!

It's just as well – because I wouldn't have known how to do it even if I had wanted to. I'd only played against him once when England beat Scotland 5–1 at Wembley. Apart from that and bits on the box I hadn't had a great deal of opportunity to study him. There has been more opportunity to play against him since I joined Liverpool.

I've faced him a few times and he is a player I admire.

He's better in the air than I am, for a start – so there's one reason why I would never have been able to do the things he did at Liverpool! But – and he has said this himself – probably his greatest attribute is his work rate. He just never stops. He has fantastic energy, but please don't think everything is down to that. He is quick, he plays good balls and he finishes well. Maybe that spell in West Germany with Hamburg made him an even better finisher than he was before. I think going to West Germany added even more confidence to his play. When you are asked to score goals then a lot is down to confidence, and Kevin has that.

I don't know if there are areas where I'm better than he is. People say I shield a ball better, or do this or that better. It doesn't really matter to me.

I was bought as Kenny Dalglish for what I had done, for what I was as a player. I wasn't bought to take over from anyone. Really, Liverpool made practically no changes in my style. That was something I was grateful for. They might have spelled it out to me that in English First Division football I wasn't only going to be an attacker, that I had to look on myself as the first line of defence too. OK, that was something I learned to accept. But that didn't involve a huge basic change to my style of play.

Maybe that's where some of the so-called secret of Liverpool lies. They don't ask players to do jobs they can't take on. All they want is for a player to do what he is best at. Plus, of course, they demand 100 per cent commitment from anyone with that red jersey on. The fans welcomed me in my first game, the Charity Shield match against Manchester United at Wembley. We drew 0–0 and they were good to me. In the next match, the first league game, we were away from home at Middlesbrough. We won and I scored, courtesy of Terry McDermott who set up the chance for me. That was the start I wanted and in the next match, at home against Newcastle United, I scored in the second half. It was at the Kop end of the ground and I nearly finished up among the fans after scoring that one. That helped kick off my relationship with the supporters. It gave me a special affinity with them, I think, because the goal was scored in front of them.

I felt at home in Liverpool from the start, because as a city it's so similar to Glasgow in so many ways. Basically industrial, basically friendly, and with the same kind of football setup – a fierce rivalry between two top clubs. In Glasgow between Celtic and Rangers and in Liverpool between ourselves and Everton. The rivalry may never get as nasty in Liverpool as it sometimes does in Glasgow but it is just as intense, believe me. You only have to be at a derby game on Merseyside to learn that.

I felt at home in Liverpool even though I spent the first eight months staying in a hotel because I couldn't find a house. I must have been off my head, and yet, it wasn't so bad. The hotel manager Jack Ferguson and his wife Meg are both Scots and they helped Marina and I settle down in the city. Staying there meant we were in the centre of town and we met a lot of people and made friends; again, that's important. Hotel life can be lonely and I've heard many players who have had to stay in hotels after being transferred complain about the isolation. When Marina came down everything was fine. We didn't have any trouble settling in at all.

It was the same at the club. I've heard of places where there are cliques and new players can be frozen out – or at least have problems fitting in – but there was nothing like that at Anfield at all. I was accepted right at the start, from the first training session I went to. You can't ask for better than that.

I was apprehensive about coming down. There's no use denying that. I was the only really new signing though Alan Hansen had signed from Partick Thistle in April, so I did wonder how things would be. I knew one or two players from playing against them for Scotland but that was all.

Then there was that goal I had scored for Scotland against England when I'd stuck it through Ray Clemence's legs. I wondered if anyone would mention it. That's all I need, I thought, for Clem to start getting stick about that goal with me two minutes in the door. There was no way I was going to say a word about it. That was in the past. Not something that I'd like to start a conversation with to a new club-mate. Yet there was John Toshack at training in the first week saying to me when we were shooting in with Clem in goal, 'Tell him you're going to aim at his legs because you've heard he's weak there!' It was the kind of dig-up you do get on the training ground or in the dressing room. But no way was I going to fall for it. 'Tosh,' I told him, 'if you want to say it, then you say it. Because there's no chance that I'll tell him that.'

Tosh was great to me and I've been delighted to see him doing well with Swansea. He took me under his wing when I first arrived and it was he who took me to see the Shanks, Liverpool's former manager the late Bill Shankly. After training one day he said to me that I should come up with him and see Shanks for a little while. It was like a pilgrimage. Tosh had been signed by Shanks and obviously he was still very close to him. I think all of the older, more experienced players at Liverpool were. They still somehow thought of Shanks as the boss because before he had retired, Bob Paisley had been the trainer.

It wasn't any lack of respect for Bob. Nothing like that, it's just that Shanks had been the gaffer for so long, and had signed so many of them, that they still had this feeling for the man. I think you always do feel close to the manager who signed you.

Anyhow, up we went to meet Shanks in the house he had just next to, of all places, the Everton training ground. I'll never forget that visit. He asked me where I was staying and I told him that I was in the Holiday Inn. Then he looked at me and in an accent that had never budged one inch from his native Ayrshire gave me two pieces of advice. 'Hotel food can be difficult for footballers, so just make sure that you don't overeat. And another thing, don't ever lose that Scottish accent!' That was the main advice he gave me. He had a tremendous personality, of course, and I think that drew the players to him.

As well as Tosh, a whole lot of the lads were good to me in all kinds of ways. When they knew I was looking for a house they would give me lifts out to see places or give me advice on areas where I might like to live. Ray Clemence, Ray Kennedy, Davie Johnson were all great to me . . . but, honestly, all the lads were fine.

Possibly the attitude at Anfield helped to make me feel as if I'd never left Celtic Park. When I joined Liverpool, they had just won the European Cup for the first time; they had won the First Division Championship yet again, and they had lost to Manchester United in the final of the English Cup. In short, they had finished the kind of season that most clubs can only dream about.

Was it enough for them? No, it wasn't enough. I learned that straightaway. Just because they had lifted the European Cup there was no way that this team would just lie back thinking over past glories. That wasn't the way they were brought up. They wanted to go on and do it again. Then they wanted to maybe win the Cup and the

League in the same season as the European Cup. Never satisfied at all. In a sense it was like Celtic. At Parkhead the pressure is always on the team for victory. It's unthinkable that you can go a season without winning a major honour. At Liverpool the players had that same feeling about them, all of it stemming from the backroom staff who have helped breed this pride into the lads.

It's not as big a backroom staff as elsewhere, maybe. It's not as well known either as far as the general public is concerned, but the Liverpool lads take some beating. The gaffer is always there, of course; then we have Ronnie Moran and Joe Fagan in charge of the training; Reuben Bennett goes to watch the opposition every week and old Tom Saunders is the man who is sent into Europe to look at the teams we are drawn against there. They all have their jobs and they do them the way the players are asked to do theirs – with 100 per cent effort for the club. Any success we have as a team has to go to them as well. They don't talk any fancy jargon at Liverpool and all the coaches who come to watch and all the camera crews who fly in from all parts of the world to try to find out the Liverpool secret tend to go away missing it altogether.

There is a continuity at the club which has served the team well down the years. The club doesn't make too many alterations to the basic style, to the basic pattern of play, and they don't make the game over-complicated. They are usually fortunate in the sense that they will have seven or eight international players in the team at any one time. I don't think people have to waste too much time talking when you have players who can think things out for themselves. And, remember, they don't keep their footballers on a tight rein at the club. The instructions given to the players are pretty basic. I think that's because they know that it's the reaction to situations on the field which is so important if a side is going to be successful.

Another thing is that almost always Liverpool think positively. The staff know when we are playing any other team in the First Division – and most sides in Europe too – that the opposition do most of the worrying. So we don't get too much advice about how the opposition play. The attitude that the gaffer has is simple: 'They are going to be more worried about how we play, so go out and let them see how we perform.'

The training we get is tough, but it isn't a whole lot different from what players get at other clubs. There is, though, a tremendous attention to detail. The training staff don't tend to worry over big matters. They know that these will be taken care of – but they worry over smaller things. They would know if there was anything wrong with any player. They'd know before one training session was over whether the lad had something on his mind or whether he was hiding an injury or whether he was worrying over a knock he had picked up. Anything at all and they would know it. Not only that, they would be able to assess whether or not it would affect his play in the next match. Ronnie and Joe are so finely tuned to each individual player and what makes each individual player tick, that they would know all this straight off. Then, when the player was leaving the training ground, they would just come up casually and say, 'What's the matter with you? What's upsetting you?' There would be no point in trying to shrug it off, saying, 'Nothing', because they just know. It's something they have learned to sense over the years they have been at the club. The gaffer oversees the training most days and he gives the team talk each week with Joe and Ronnie chipping in.

They don't just sit quietly. If there is a point to be made, then they'll make it.

It blends quite naturally into a teamwork off the park which I feel is reflected in the teamwork on the park. There isn't any secret formula, unless a deep and thorough knowledge of the players at the club is a secret formula. Plus, of course, a deep and thorough knowledge of the game itself.

They usually start off, too, with good material to handle. It boils down to this: everyone goes to school but not everyone is as academic as the next person, and it's the same in football. They tell us what to do and we go out to try to do it – but if a player didn't have it in the first place then they could talk until they were blue in the face and it wouldn't make any difference. At Liverpool they start with the best of basic materials, or as near to the best as it's possible to get. Just about a whole team of international players on occasions . . .

If there are off-the-field problems, the club is always ready to take care of them. The secretary Peter Robinson is there, the chairman Mr Smith is there, and the gaffer is there; you can go to any one of them. Whatever the problem, one of these three will help you solve it. They will spend time sorting out individual problems because they know that if they have a happy player then they are going to get more out of him on the park. They look on Liverpool as their family and nothing is too much trouble for them. Honestly, there is no way I'd ever want to leave the club.

I realize that one day it will end – when Liverpool decide that I'm not doing the job that they want from me. As a professional footballer I accept that. It's going to be a sad day, though, because I haven't had one ounce of worry since I made the move south from Celtic. Any player who asked me for advice would be told, 'Get to Liverpool if you have the chance.' As far as I'm concerned there isn't a club like this anywhere else in the world.

Even the Continent would never have lured me away from Anfield. Kevin went and I admired him for that because he put his neck on the chopping block to a certain extent. A year before the move he said that he wanted to go abroad and that might have rebounded on him. It didn't and he was a success at Hamburg. Good luck to him. The same goes for my Scotland mate Joe Jordan. When he left Manchester United for AC Milan Joe must have known he was taking a chance. He's about the same age as myself and it's not the best time to move to a totally new environment. Joe did, and when I saw him with the Scotland squad not long after the move, he was happy that he had gone to the Continent. It's not for me, though. I've got enough problems in the Anfield dressing room making them understand my English, so how would it be in West Germany or in Italy? Seriously, I've just never had the desire to leave Liverpool. I've achieved most of my ambitions with the club and they have looked after me – that's all you can look for as a player.

I suppose I've been lucky too in having Bob Paisley as manager. People always ask about our gaffer because they can't quite believe that the Bob Paisley they see on the telly is the same man as the one who has won three European Cups. I'm not surprised – because honestly the gaffer is the same with us as he is on the box. It's not an act or anything – he's just that way. He doesn't want any fuss or anything. The lads have told me that he didn't even want the job when the Shanks retired. He was happy being the trainer and he didn't want to take on anything else.

It's a strange thing about him and about the Shanks,

too. He could have been living in a really big house, like other managers have had, with a swimming pool, the lot. He doesn't though and neither did the Shanks. I think they both stayed in the same houses they always had. Nothing fancy. Just the kind of house they needed and no more than that. Change the accents, and there aren't any big differences between Bob and Shanks. They come from the same backgrounds – Shanks from a mining village in Ayrshire, Bob from a mining village in County Durham. I think they learned their sense of values in those mining communities and these have never changed in spite of all the success they have known as managers. They never forgot their backgrounds and I look on that as a bit of a lesson to all of us. It's easy to get carried away – but they didn't. Also, neither is the type to let the players get too carried away either. Of course, the Shanks led by example, as does Bob Paisley now. 'Remember, there's always work to be done!' is a vital part of the Anfield philosophy.

It's fairly typical of Bob Paisley that although he could have a Jaguar if he wanted one, he won't because it's too symbolic. He sees them as being flash. He could have any car he wanted but, though he did have a Rover for a while, he drives a Granada Ghia. He just doesn't like fuss or too much glamour or anything like that.

Basically I think Bob's always happiest when he is out on the training ground kicking a ball about. The training staff still take on the younger players every morning we train and a senior player like myself coming back after injury might be privileged to guest with them. The Boss is always in goal.

People ask me how it is that I get on with him so well and I just reply, 'Because I don't speak to him much.' And that's true! I don't remember having had any really prolonged conversation with the gaffer in the years I've been at Anfield. I certainly haven't had any disputes or rows with him. We've talked about football, and that's about it. Hs did ask me once what a Rover was like, because I was driving one at the time. But even when it comes down to contracts, he just tells players that a new contract is upstairs. If there are any worries they talk them out with the club secretary Peter Robinson. I get a little bit of stick at times from the lads when he has come out and said something good about me. I'll get a chorus of 'My Kenny, my Kenny' when I go into the dressing room – but I think he praises all his players. Though he can hand out stick if he has to! All of us know that because we've all heard him from time to time. But really he is a very honest man and a man without any airs and graces. He doesn't get bogged down in too many technicalities when he gives a team talk. He tells us what he expects from us and that's about it. I know that it all must sound too simple, too easy, but that is honestly the way it works. Despite people saying we are stereotyped, we are allowed quite a bit of freedom inside the team pattern. We're encouraged to play off-the-cuff when the opportunity arises.

Many viewers saw Bob Paisley on the box in Paris complaining that he couldn't get black pudding for breakfast; that's just the man as he is. I don't think there is anything bad you could say about him. He's just a nice man. I've hit it off with him, I don't know of any special reasons why, except that he is a thoroughly nice man.

He has the knack too of spotting things that might be wrong with the team or with a player and then just quietly making a wee comment which sorts it out. He doesn't do it in any big deal way, he just walks alongside and has a word in the player's ear. Or maybe he mentions something generally in a team talk. It may not sound much at the time, but generally I find he has summed everything up with one of those homely phrases he uses so often. Three European Cup wins haven't changed him and I don't think that anything would.

4

Days with the Doc

The way I started my international career was important
. . . because I genuinely believe that I played my first
game for Scotland just when the national team was
kicking off a massive revival.

It was fortunate for me that I broke through when
Tommy Docherty was the man in charge of the side,
because the Doc revolutionized international football in
Scotland. There is absolutely no doubt in my mind about
that.

He blew away the cobwebs which had hung around the
international setup. He possibly upset some of the more
old-fashioned officials at the Scottish Football Association, but to the players he was marvellous.

I mentioned before that players feel an affinity for the
manager who signed them for a club. In the same way I
feel an affinity for Tommy Doc because one November
night in 1971 he gave me the start to my international
career. I was surprised to hear that I was in the squad.
That was really my first full season in Celtic's League side
and we had only gone a few months into the season. I had
picked up Under-23 caps before under the previous
Scotland boss Bobby Brown but I didn't expect to get such
an early call from the Doc. He was a caretaker boss at that
time, put in charge for our two remaining European
championship matches against Portugal and Belgium. The
matches meant nothing because we had failed to qualify
by that time and Bobby Brown had lost the job he had
held down for some years.

The Doc had just come back to British football from Portugal where he had been in charge at Oporto. Terry Neill, now with Arsenal, was manager of Hull and made Tommy his assistant. It was from there that he handled Scotland on a part-time basis for two games. The first was against Portugal at Hampden, where the Scots won 2–1 against a good side which still included Eusebio. The crowd was huge, thanks to the Doc building interest in the game.

Then it was on to Pittodrie for the second match against Belgium. Belgium too had a good side, with Paul Van Himst of Anderlecht still so influential for them. I think the SFA must have been sorry that game had been switched from Hampden. They had realized it was meaningless and settled for a game at Aberdeen, little knowing the impact that the Doc would have. Again he sold the game, and this time it was a 40,000 sellout.

To go back a bit – when I was told I was in the pool of players I was in Malta with Celtic. We were there to play Sliema Wanderers in the second round of the European Cup and I was lying by the pool when our boss Jock Stein came up to give me the news. 'You're in the Scotland pool,' he told me. 'Congratulations.' It seemed so matter-of-fact – but I really could scarcely grasp it. It wasn't something I had expected. But then, the Doc always tried to give young players a chance at club level and here he was doing the same with the Scotland side. I was delighted. You could sense that the international setup was ready to explode, that the Doc was going to make the Scotland side mean something once again after so many years in the wilderness.

Just to be a part of it, at the start of it all, was something special. I didn't play from the start in the Belgium game. It was just after half time when I went on to replace Alex

Cropley, who was then with Hibs. We won the game 1–0 with wee Jimmy Johnstone chipping the ball over for John O'Hare to head the goal. Then Steve Murray was very unlucky with a smashing diving header which went just past. I know that wee Jinky, Jimmy Johnstone, was very special that night. The Belgians couldn't stop him. That's about all I remember about the game. It's hard to look back and recall much more – but maybe it was just that the occasion was too much for me to take in.

The next game was in Amsterdam at the Olympic stadium against Holland who, two years or so later, were to be in the final of the World Cup against West Germany. We lost that one 2–1 with George Graham scoring our goal; little Archie Gemmill just missed giving us a draw near the end. But the defeat didn't matter so much – we were on our way. Though there was a considerable hiccup which could have stopped my career under the Doc if he had been vindictive about it.

Scotland were invited to play in a mini World Cup tournament in Brazil in the summer of 1972. The Doc wanted me to go, along with my Celtic team-mates Davie Hay and Lou Macari. Our club boss Jock Stein didn't want us to go. He felt that by the time the summer came around we would have had enough football. I was young then and it was the end of my first full season with Celtic. I'd played a lot of games and I decided to go along with the club view and stay at home.

To be fair to the club, I was tired – it was touch and go whether I'd play for them in the Scottish Cup final against Hibs that year. In the end only Lou Macari went on the trip from Celtic. Now I often wish I had gone because the lads who went told us just how great the team spirit had been. It was another five years before I had the chance of playing in South America, and in particular of playing against Brazil in the Maracana stadium.

That was the first time a Scottish international team went to South America. It was typical of the Doc that he should fight for that trip and get it, and even obtain a more or less scratch team to go out and do well. There were a bundle of call-offs, yet the team drew with Yugoslavia and Czechoslovakia and only lost to Brazil by a late Jairzinho goal after George Graham had hit the bar.

When the Doc came back it would have been easy for him to leave out the players who hadn't gone, but he stood by me. When the World Cup campaign started with two games against Denmark, I was in the squad each time, coming on as a substitute in Copenhagen where we won 4–1 and then playing and scoring when we beat them 2–0 at Hampden. A month or so later the Doc was off to Manchester United.

Yet his contribution towards the international scene in Scotland had been magnificent. He helped rebuild the setup. For the first time the youth team and the Under-23 team were given importance, because he knew that's where the players of the future would come from. He had a Second Division select for which he arranged games and he was usually there to boost the lads. He gave a lot of the players in the Scottish game something extra to play for. He recognized lads in the Second Division and gave them a chance when other managers would have concentrated their talent-spotting only on the glamour games. He looked at some of the unfashionable clubs, saw players with ability there and brought them into the limelight.

What's more, he rekindled interest in the national team when that enthusiasm could have gone into decline. I think it's fair to say that the Scots are more patriotic as regards their national team than the English are. I would make the same point about the Irish and the Welsh. The populations of these nations are smaller and the team becomes the focal point of ambitions much more easily. It isn't that way in England, probably because of its size and probably because the people in the north won't travel to Wembley the way our own punters will. The Doc gave all these Scots fans new hope. He knew how they felt and he fed all their patriotic feelings. His way was to tell the world that Scotland had more than her fair share of world-class players. 'Open a cupboard door up in Glasgow,' he used to say, 'and another good player will fall out.' The fans wanted to believe that and they chanted his name from the Hampden terraces as he guided the team to good, solid results. Suddenly too the game against England wasn't the only one which counted. The Doc had been out in the big wide world and he knew that if we persisted in believing that winning over England was all that mattered, we would lose our way. He emphasized time and again that the World Cup was the biggest target of all for the national side. His two wins over Denmark helped us get to the finals for the first time since he was a player.

It had been back in 1958 in Sweden, when the Doc was in the Scotland squad and we last played in the World Cup finals. Team after team had failed in the intervening period, good teams among them. Now, with the two wins over Denmark, and with our other section rivals Czechoslovakia dropping a point in Copenhagen, only a win at Hampden against the Czechs was needed for us to reach West Germany.

That was one of the legacies the Doc left behind him when he went to Manchester United. Others were the increasing importance given to the youth and Under-23 – now Under-21 – teams, and the impetus he gave the game by making the international side so important again.

I loved having him as manager. The spirit about the teams when the Doc was in charge was tremendous. You never felt ill at ease, never felt that there was any friction. He kept everyone going, of course. I loved his jokes and his Glasgow patter. I still do. Like the quip about Derek Parlane when Rangers said – meaning it in money – 'Two hundred thousand wouldn't buy him,' and the Doc cracked, 'And I'm one of the two hundred thousand.'

Obviously I was disappointed that the Doc left the job. I think he brought professionalism to the squad. He made us believe in ourselves and he was a marvellous motivator. He probably got the best out of wee Jimmy Johnstone in the games in which he used him. He believed in skill and he believed in attack. He brought Denis Law back and gave Willie Morgan his chance, and he always wanted his teams to enjoy their football.

It was hard to do anything else when he was around. They were good times and it was a pity they didn't last long. But when he was offered the Manchester United job who could blame him for taking it? It is one of the biggest jobs in the country and he was the man Old Trafford needed. He did have difficult times there but those supporters loved him and he loved them. United have found it very difficult to get someone to replace him and even sacked his successor.

I know he has had a lot of bad breaks recently and people think of him as a bit of a rogue, but I like him. And I know that he'll never be beaten. He keeps bouncing back and I think some of that spirit has rubbed off on every team he handled.

The Doc has charisma. Something he has never lost even during his troubles over the last few years. Whenever the Doc walked into a room, or a restaurant, or anywhere at all, I would hear people saying, 'There's the Doc, there's the Doc.' He had that kind of dominating personality and that's what Scottish football needed at the time when he took over.

He took Denis Law on that Brazilian tour and then Willie Ormond brought him in for the World Cup games in 1974. That was great because Denis Law was the best player Scotland ever had. He'd always been my hero when I was a kid. Not for anything he did with Manchester United, but for what he did for Scotland. He was every youngster's idol, and rightly so. When I was in the squad with him for the first time, I was in awe of him. Not because of anything he said or did but just because of the memories I had of him from the time I was a youngster going along to Hampden to watch him. There was never any big-time thing about Denis when he was in the Scotland squad. He was always just the same as any of the lads. As long as he could get a pot of tea in the afternoons then he was happy. That was him quite pleased with life. He didn't need anything elaborate, just that pot of tea and a few of the lads around to have a blether. He is a tremendous guy and was a great, great player. I do think it's sad that he doesn't really have anything to show for that cap record he held for so long except maybe for a presentation from some of the lads and something from Rod Stewart. I suppose everyone – or nearly everyone – sees their records broken, but I felt sad that I should break that one. It seemed wrong somehow.

I can remember being with Celtic and playing in Bobby Charlton's testimonial match at Old Trafford. More than 50,000 people were there, and at the end I sprinted towards Denis just like any fan in that crowd, because I wanted to have his jersey! I really sprinted to make sure that I reached him first. I said, 'Excuse me, Denis, but do you think I could have your jersey?' He said it was OK

and I said, 'Thanks very much,' and up that tunnel I went
and into the dressing room and the jersey, number eight –
I think Brian Kidd had the number ten that night – was
tucked away down at the bottom of my bag.

So there we were sitting around just getting ourselves
ready when big Jock Stein, came in and said, 'OK, let's
have all these jerseys because they are being auctioned for
charity.'

I nearly died. I just told him, 'I'm sorry but that jersey is
mine. If I have to pay for it then I'll do it. But no one is
going to take it away from me.'

I meant it too. Denis Law had given that jersey to me
and I wasn't going to part with it. In the end I kept it and I
didn't have to pay – but no matter what it had cost I would
have paid up. That's what Denis Law meant to me.

5

Wee Willie and the first time in the World Cup finals

It was another St Valentine's Day Massacre that night at Hampden when Willie Ormond took over the Scotland team for the first time. The trouble was that we were on the receiving end of the massacre and Willie Ormond, later to be nicknamed Wee Donny by all the players, was the new boss who had to suffer while England – of all teams – hammered five goals in against us.

It was a frosty night and a miserable night for all the team. Hampden was hard, possibly unplayable, but this was an international to celebrate the Scottish FA's centenary and so the game went ahead. We all wished it hadn't.

Ninety minutes later we trooped off the field to see our new gaffer in the dressing rooms after being humiliated by an England team that still contained three of their World Cup winners, Bobby Moore, Alan Ball and Martin Peters. I don't make any excuses about the weather conditions when I look back now. That would be wrong. They were bad, but they were the same for the English lads. It was just a bad, bad night for us from the opening goal we lost – an own goal by Peter Lorimer of Leeds United – right through the other four scored by Allan Clarke (2), Mike Channon and Martin Chivers.

There couldn't have been a more disastrous start for any team manager, yet now I think it was a blessing in disguise. There was no way any of us could have seen that at the time. We were all too sick to see anything other than that depressing 5–0 result. But I'm sure that those of the lads who stayed on, tried their very best to repay the wee man for letting him down that first night. And we did let him down. There is no doubt about that. Ormond had stepped up from St Johnstone, a small provincial club which he had taken into Europe and turned into title challengers. But to the lads from down south he was an unknown. Even for the homebased players like myself it wasn't easy to find out much about him. The record at Perth told you something. Yet statistics can never tell players enough about a team boss.

After the Doc, who had been larger than life, Wee Willie was a complete contrast. Quiet, shy really, and completely unassuming. Half the time you would never have known he was there. So when he took over I suppose we were on trial with him and he was possibly in the same position. Remember, when Wee Willie took command he needed a win at Hampden over the Czechs to reach West Germany and take Scotland to the finals for the first time since 1958. That was very much in all our minds when Tommy Docherty left to join Manchester United.

When I make the point that the players didn't know Wee Willie too well, it has to be said that he didn't know the Anglos too well either. In fact, a few of them he had never seen play apart from on the box. But the great thing we found out was that Willie Ormond was ready to learn the things he had to learn. He began making long trips down to England to see as many games and as many players as possible. He made up his mind that there had to be one or two changes. Several players didn't play for him again after the debacle against England. When he made up his mind, he followed through. He began to build the kind of team he wanted and by the time we played in our first match in the World Cup finals in West Germany, just under eighteen months after that first game, he had made eight changes in personnel. Yet once a player was in the team he was the most loyal gaffer imaginable. He stuck by players when they were having a bad time, defended them from criticism if he felt they should be defended and generally was a really popular manager.

It was Willie Ormond who brought Denis Law back for the qualifying game against Czechoslovakia at Hampden. It was Willie Ormond who gave Tommy Hutchison his first cap that same night when big Hutch was the star of the whole game. It was Willie Ormond who gave Joe Jordan and Jim Holton their international starts.

And it was Willie Ormond who helped me a lot in those early days with the Scotland team. I was a bit in awe of a lot of the more famous players in the team. I've told you how I felt about Denis Law and it was the same with Billy Bremner – I got his jersey too when we played Leeds in Jackie Charlton's testimonial – and some of the others. Let's face it, I was just starting out on my international career and at club level although I had been with Celtic I was still in awe of players who had been in the game so much longer. In those days with the national squad I sat quietly and listened a lot. There was no way I was going to push myself in. It was different at club level even though the players there might be as big names as those with Scotland. At Celtic Park you were meeting the players every day and you became familiar with them because these were the people you were working alongside all the time.

Willie Ormond looked after me. Only once did I ever feel let down by him and that was when I was heading for a record in consecutive appearances for Scotland. I was on the verge of beating the record which had been held by George Young the former Scotland and Rangers captain when the wee man left me sitting on the bench for the match at Hampden against Wales in 1976. That would have been my thirty-fourth consecutive game for Scotland, but even when two players took knocks he didn't put me on. I was upset about that, really disappointed, and I've never known why he did it. He knew the record was on for me. Everyone had known it before the game and it had taken a long time, obviously, to string that number of matches together. It's happened since and I now do hold the record but it should have happened on that night at Hampden when we beat the Welsh 3–1.

In the end though, I didn't hold any grudges because Wee Donny wasn't the kind of man you could hold any against. He was essentially an honest person and he wanted honesty from the players who were under him. I think his popularity with the players was one of his strengths. In saying that, I mean that he inspired loyalty in the squad. The team spirit at that time was tremendous, much better than it was to be four years later in Argentina. The lads liked the manager and got on well with each other. There was something about Willie Ormond which got through to you. He didn't go in for long involved talks about the games you were going into. He went to see the opposition and he briefed you but he did it in plain down-to-earth terms which footballers immediately understood. He also had the knack of picking the right players. People doubted him when he brought back Denis Law – yet the emotional impact Denis had at Hampden that night helped carry the team to the finals. People criticized Ormond when he used Jim Holton at centre half – but the wee man knew what he wanted. He was looking for an old-fashioned reliable stopper. Big Jim gave him solidity there, and during the West German finals the big fellow became a hero to the fans. That doesn't happen often to defenders.

Willie Ormond was also willing to give players their heads – up to a point. He knew the pattern he wanted us to use but encouraged us to express ourselves within that basic framework. The relationship between him and the captain Billy Bremner was good for Scotland. Willie was quiet, but wee Billy was forceful. While Willie coaxed the best out of players, Billy would tongue-lash them. They were a contrast in styles, and that difference was marvellous for the squad. They were a perfect pairing.

Billy was always ready to take on responsibility as captain. On the field he ran things at Leeds and he came to do the same for Scotland. He attracted criticism because he was always ready to drive players on, always ready to demand greater efforts from them. Sometimes it worked, sometimes it didn't. Billy was hard on players. He had a rough tongue and he demanded a lot from the other lads in the team. Yet Billy never asked more from anyone than he asked from himself. He set high standards in his own play and he wanted other players to live up to these. He thought a lot about the game; it was Billy and big George Graham who used to work out free kicks and other set pieces for us at training. We relied on them a lot for that kind of thing. I suppose we relied on Billy too for his leadership. It's easy for people to snipe at him now because he slowed the pace of our opening game in West Germany against Zaire. It wasn't an easy decision to make on the night – but Billy didn't jib at it. He did what he thought was right and I wouldn't have argued with him that night in Dortmund.

We won 2–0 with goals from Peter Lorimer and Joe Jordan getting us through – but it was a game we could have lost. Early on it seemed sewn up, then they came hurling back at us and we were already in trouble when Billy decided to slow things down. We might easily have lost that match, and reactions then would have been even worse.

I'll get to that later but, looking back at that World Cup, when everything was so new to all of us, it's difficult to realize that we went there under a bit of a cloud. Everything that could go wrong – off the field – seemed to go wrong. We were let down badly in a perks deal which had been supposedly set up for us. Talk of half a million pounds for the squad fell flat and we all suffered. Then we were criticized because people thought we were chasing money, more interested in cash than playing for Scotland. That was just nonsense. When any team qualifies for a World Cup there is an immediate spin-off in perks for the players. That is bound to happen. Part of the trouble was that we didn't know how to handle it, and we had an agent appointed by the Scottish FA whom none of the lads had met.

Imagine. There we were at our headquarters down the Clyde coast at Largs, preparing for the World Cup on the eve of our departure for West Germany, and we had to meet our agent to ask him to explain why things were falling down around us.

Predictably, things didn't work out – but let me say this. Not one of those players who were in West Germany could have worked harder than they did for their country. Their minds weren't on money when they were training and working and playing out there. Their minds were on winning and on trying to make the Scottish supporters who were there, and those who were back home, proud of them. It's as simple as that. The money aspect always crops up. It can't be ignored because the World Cup is big business these days. If some of the huge amounts of money invested in advertising can be earned by the players then I don't see anything wrong with that. All that's needed is for someone to handle it properly. We didn't have that and in the end we didn't make much money at all. I can't remember the exact amounts because these varied from player to player, but no one made any fortunes. In the end most of the boys were laughing at the whole affair. They couldn't even get angry.

The other problems which hit us were brought on by some of the lads having a bit of fun and being caught out. From what I can gather Scotland teams have always had their share of high-spirited players – and our squad was no exception. Yet, again I think that too much was made of the incidents. If we'd been a touring rugby team it would have all been put down to a bit of fun – a football team and it becomes a pretty serious affair. I'll never understand why.

The first problem was when a bunch of the players had a couple of beers after the British championship match against Wales. We had won the game 2–0, it was a Tuesday night and when we got back down to Largs late on, the Boss said that the players could have a drink. We had the England game coming up on the Saturday but no one saw harm in having a drink on a Tuesday. Nor was there – but the celebrations got out of hand. My Celtic team-mate wee Jimmy Johnstone got himself involved. He was always a cert, the wee man, to get rolled up in any trouble that was going. I was in bed when it all happened and I was wakened by my room-mate Danny McGrain who told me, 'Wee Jimmy's out there on the river in a boat . . .'

I couldn't believe it. I thought I was having my leg pulled, but when I eventually looked out of the window there was the wee man floating out to sea, waving an oar above his head and singing his head off. How on earth, I thought, are they going to get him back in? Some of the other players thought the same and tried to launch another boat. Luckily for them it sank before they could get very far. There we were, the Scotland World Cup squad, with the star winger adrift in a rowing boat, a few others sinking close to shore and the manager wondering what else could happen.

What did happen was that the coastguards had to go out to rescue wee Jimmy and the news was blasted around the country a few hours later. You should have seen that wee man the next day! Wee Jimmy took it bad when he had done anything remotely out of order. The day after – or rather, later the same day – he knew he was in bother and he worried himself sick about it. Then, when it mattered most, out on the park against England on the Saturday, we beat them 2–0. The fans forgave him then and so did Willie Ormond, who was first onto the field to hug wee Jimmy, the hero of the match.

Within two weeks he was the villain again when he got in bother along with Billy Bremner. Again, as far as I was concerned, it was exaggerated. The two of them were having a few drinks in our hotel in Norway before one of the warm-up games. We had lost to Belgium 2–1 in Bruges and then travelled by charter to Oslo for the next match. There were a few days before the next match against the Norwegians and the lads thought it would be OK to relax a bit. There was a wee bit of bother and the affair finished with both of them almost being sent home. All this – and we hadn't set foot in West Germany yet!

Yet we won 2–1 against Norway. I scored, Joe Jordan got the other and somehow, almost the way it was after that opening defeat when wee Donny joined us, the lads closed ranks. You get that at times. When players feel that they're in trouble they get together more. The incident helped the team spirit, which had been strong in any case.

After that the lads became more and more determined to do well. The other thing which is worth remembering is that once the lads got to West Germany there wasn't a hint of bother from anyone. They got to that hotel, the Erbismuhle up in the hills outside Frankfurt, and they worked as hard as any squad of players who were in those finals. Any carry-on they might have had at Largs or in Norway was over. Wee Donny would tell you that himself.

Basically we were a bit unlucky in the way the draw had given us Zaire to begin with. As it was their first match, they would be playing out of their skins, and it was the one match where we were understandably nervous. The last team from Scotland which had played in the World Cup had been sixteen years earlier when I was about eight years old. People like Tommy Docherty and Bobby Evans and Tommy Younger were in our squad. So there was a bit of pressure on us. Then too, we were a little bit naive. Our team just wanted to go out and beat everyone in sight, to play normally, and just win the games, not consider how best we might benefit from draws, for example. The Brazilians, shrewdest of all at this level, had already reckoned that goal difference could take a team into the quarter-finals. Their reasoning was that the team who scored most against Zaire would top the group and the next highest scorers would be second. They themselves settled for that second spot.

Predictably, the opening game had been played to a 0–0 draw between the Brazilians and Yugoslavia.

On the Friday night in Dortmund we had to face the Africans from Zaire. To start with things went as expected . . . in fact better than anyone hoped. After only thirty-three minutes we were two goals ahead, thanks to a Leeds United combination. Ths first one arrived in twenty-seven minutes when Joe Jordan headed the ball down to his team-mate Peter Lorimer who blasted a spectacular goal. Six minutes later Billy Bremner hoisted a free kick into the Zaire goal and there was big Joe again to head the second.

But after that Zaire came back at us with a lot of skill and courage. There were times when we were in difficulty. But we held on to the lead and then prepared to meet Brazil. The Slavs hit nine goals against poor Zaire, softened up by us in that first game which they had put so much into.

Meanwhile, in what everyone considered one of the best games of the 1974 finals, we drew with Brazil 0–0. We came desperately close to beating Brazil. Once, late in the game, the ball struck Billy Bremner's legs as he raced in on goal and then bounced on the wrong side of the post. That could have taken us through.

In a sense the Brazilians were a disappointment because they were so physical. Mario Zagalo had decided to play a European style game – what he meant was a physical game. Willie Ormond exploded after the match and told the world's press, 'Every one of my players has bruises and cuts to show for that ninety minutes. Brazil were a disgrace.' It was not the kind of game we expected from the country which had produced Pele.

But then they had expected to face rough stuff in West Germany and reacted by dishing it out themselves. They still had good players – Rivelino was outstanding for one – but it was not the Brazil we all remembered. It was just another World Cup lesson for the novices from Scotland.

A few days later we met Yugoslavia and drew 1–1 with them, while the Brazilians scored the three they required against the Africans. The newspapers had built up the Yugoslavs, suggesting them as a probable threat to the

West Germans, and they did have good players, especially in midfield where Oblak and Osim both played superbly. They were also in a better position than us as it turned out, because of their goal feast against Zaire. To go through, we had to win.

But the Yugoslavs didn't allow us to play, and when Karasi scored for them with only nine minutes remaining, it looked as if we would go out sadly. But Joe Jordan struck again in the last minute and that equalizer had us waiting for the other result. If Brazil had not scored a third goal then we would have marched on with the Slavs. But it was not to be. What hurt us most that night was the third Brazil goal. The ball should have been saved, but somehow the Zaire keeper made a hash of it and it trickled over the line in the closing minutes. That's what finally beat us.

The fans, who had taken over Frankfurt for the two weeks or so that we were there, stayed behind to cheer. A few tears were shed by them, but they still stood around that bus to cheer every one of the players as we went on board and headed for Erbismuhle and our own wake.

I can't mention the supporters without saying how much we all think of them. There were ten or fifteen thousand people over from Scotland for these matches and they were great. The Germans loved them. They really did. Tartan was everywhere in Frankfurt for those two weeks and we appreciated the support we had. Mind you, I've never played anywhere without some Scots being there. It hasn't mattered where it has been in the world. Even in Iron Curtain countries like Hungary or Rumania or Poland, when the matches haven't been so terribly important, someone has been there to support us. Sometimes the fans have been given a bad name, but the majority of the people who watch Scotland and who travel the world to see us play have been tremendous ambassadors. We know now to look for them no matter where we have a game.

We did have a wake up there in the hills and Rod Stewart sang for us before he broke down in tears. There were a few tears shed that night and I felt a very real regret which still gnaws away at me. In the three matches there I didn't think I played well enough, I'd let down the manager and the other lads. That's how I felt then, and I still feel that maybe I should have done better. Or even that I could have done better. Maybe I wasn't ready for these finals. I was overawed by some of the other, older players in the squad and there were occasions when I was frightened to try things in case they wouldn't come off. Another regret is that I can scarcely remember any of the games in detail. They're all part of the blur which surrounds those first finals I played in.

One memory, however, which will last forever is of the welcome waiting for us at Glasgow Airport when we arrived back a couple of days later. Thousands of people were there, flags were flying, banners were waving and we had to fight our way through crowds who had managed somehow to get onto the tarmac. We hadn't qualified, but we had not let the people back home down. They just wanted to tell us that in their own very special way and we all appreciated it. It was a very emotional homecoming.

For wee Jimmy Johnstone it was to be his only World Cup finals, and he was kept on the bench. So one of the really rare talents in Scottish football never kicked a ball on the game's greatest stage. That was a tragedy – for the game as much as for the wee man. He was unbelievable as a player. Honestly, it's wrong that he should be remembered for the troubles he got himself into. At least it's wrong if the main thing about him, his talent, isn't mentioned as well. There are dozens of stories about wee Jimmy, he is that type of fellow. But no one could play like him. He's the only player I've seen who could beat men without touching the ball, without a single touch. He'd stand there with the ball in front of him and just sway his hips and the opponent would fall for that and the wee man had left him behind. He was very sharp too, and he could sustain his game right through a hard ninety minutes. I'm not just meaning he was sharp on the ball, by the way, though obviously he was that. I'm meaning sharp upstairs too, because when he was carrying that ball forward he knew exactly what he was going to do. Players just couldn't cope with him when he was on song. It was marvellous to watch him. Yet he always gives credit to Bobby Murdoch, who played behind him for Celtic. He told me once, 'Without Bobby in there behind me I would only have been half the player I was.' He really loved Bobby. But the wee man himself was unique. No one I've ever played with has been as talented with the ball. He was a marvellous player and people should remember him for that, instead of just thinking about him sailing down the Clyde in a rowboat!

6

We join Ally's army

Ally Macleod stormed onto the Scottish international scene just before the beginning of the British international championship in 1977. Eighteen months later he had gone, back to club management after a reign which saw us reach the finals of the World Cup once more . . . then crash out of these Argentina games in disgrace.

Ally's reign was short. But it was evenful. Like Tommy Docherty he was in complete contrast to the quiet man, Willie Ormond, who had guided us to the previous finals . . . and to a defeat in them which was at least honourable.

Strangely, Ally the extrovert manager stepped gingerly into the job, in stark contrast to his one-man publicity machine that we had seen at Ayr United and Aberdeen and would be able to watch more closely at international level.

We were to open the British championships with a match at Wrexham where we had to face Wales, who would be crucial World Cup opponents in the months ahead. Ally didn't intend to start with a defeat. Nor did he intend to give the Welshmen any ideas on how he might approach the job once he had settled into it. So he opted for a 4–4–2 setup, one which was designed to pack the midfield and smother the Welsh attackers. Ally made no bones about it. This was a game where avoiding defeat was essential.

The tactics used that day to get a 0–0 draw were not nice to watch. They didn't please the fans who had travelled to see the game. They didn't please some of the players, who muttered against them behind the scenes. To be fair, they weren't the kind of tactics that Ally wanted the Scottish team to use.

We soon learned that, with two wins in succession giving Ally the dream start which had eluded poor Willie Ormond when he took over! After Wrexham we moved back to Hampden for a midweek game with Northern Ireland which we won 3–0, with Gordon McQueen scoring once and me managing to get the others. So the stage was set for the biennial clash with England at Wembley. It's always the number one event on the football calendar for Scottish fans. Just as the English fans look on the Cup final as the great day of each season, the Scots look on the clash with England as the big one. When it's at Wembley, it's even bigger than the Hampden match.

A year before we had won at Hampden with Don Masson and myself helping the team to a 2–1 win. Now we wanted a repeat, especially as our last visit to London had finished with us losing 5–1. Well, this time we won 2–1. Gordon McQueen and I shared the goals again, and the fans decided to share the goalposts. And the nets. And the sacred Wembley turf and anything else they could lay their hands on as souvenirs. We didn't see much of it because we had to flee for the dressing rooms, though I'm told that Rod Stewart was on the pitch that day. He is one of the team's most fervent supporters.

We met Rod Stewart first before the World Cup finals in 1974, when he came down to visit the team at Largs. I was in bed one afternoon when John Blackley came upstairs to waken me and Danny McGrain, who was my roommate. He told us Rod Steward was downstairs, but we didn't believe it at first. There he was though, ready to make up a special presentation to Denis Law who was

Scotland's most capped player at the time. Now he turns
up at as many of our games as he can. When he can't get
to the matches he tries to arrange a link to Hampden or
wherever by telephone from Los Angeles, where he lives,
and has a journalist commentate for him. That's the way
Scots fans are.

The Wembley victory gave Ally the platform he had
always wanted and gave the team a springboard for our
tour of South America. This was the first three-country
tour Scotland had made. Their one and only time in South
America before had been to Brazil in 1972 – the trip I
didn't go on with Tommy Docherty's squad. This latest
one had been planned because the World Cup finals were
in Argentina the following summer and it would be useful
as an acclimatization trip *if* we managed to qualify once
again.

Our success continued for most of the trip. We started
in Chile and won there 4–2. I scored once, Lou Macari
twice and Asa Hartford snatched the other goal. On to
Buenos Aires where we drew with the hosts of the 1978
World Cup 1–1, thanks to a Don Masson penalty. Poor
Willie Johnston was sent off in this match for nothing, a
hint of what we could expect the following summer at the
World Cup finals.

That apart, we returned home having suffered just one
solitary defeat – 2–0 against Brazil in Rio. We lost our
next game too, the first of the next season. That was a
warm-up for us in East Berlin; the East Germans beat us
1–0, but we played well and there were signs that the
team's confidence was rising as we approached our World
Cup game with the Czechs at Hampden.

That was just two weeks after our match in East Berlin.
We had lost our opening match against the Czechs in
Prague 2–0 when Willie Ormond was still in command,

and had Andy Gray sent off. Then we had beaten the other team in our group, Wales, 1–0 in our home match. When Ally took over we had two games to go, and in the meantime, the Welsh had defeated the Czechs 3–0 in Wrexham. The door to Argentina was open!

We won the return match with the Czechs. We won it so well, in fact, that the veteran West German team manager Helmut Schoen took a film of the game back home with him to show to his players. He was quoted at the time as saying 'This is the way that the modern game must be played. Teams must show the aggression of the Scots, and the speed and the skill of the Scots.'

Certainly the Czechs couldn't live with us that night; Joe Jordan, Asa Harford and I scored the goals in our 3–1 win. All we had to do now was beat the Welsh in our last section game and we were in Argentina . . .

That game had its own share of controversy attached to it, before and during the so vital ninety minutes. Before the game there was disagreement over the Welsh Football Association decision to transfer the game to Anfield – now my home ground – because crowd restrictions at either Cardiff or Wrexham would limit the gate severely. They realized that with our fans swarming down over the border they had a sellout on their hands. Also they could have faced a lot of potential crowd trouble if they hadn't found a suitable ground.

I doubt if I've ever, since then, known ticket fever quite the way it was for that match. Naturally I was inundated with ticket requests from home; there I was, a Liverpool player, and the game was at Anfield. The Scots fans were even travelling down to the Welsh FA headquarters in Wrexham to buy tickets there. Really, Liverpool isn't too far away from North Wales and so the Welsh did expect that their fans would rival the tartan army. At the ground as the game approached, Joey Jones and John Toshack – both Welsh international players as well as my Liverpool team-mates – were telling me that their supporters would outnumber any we could bring with us.

I'll never forget going to Anfield that night and seeing the sea of tartan which seemed to surround the terraces and stands. Then out we went onto the park. I saw big Joey look towards the Kop, where he predicted that the Welsh would rule, and wince at the tartan which had flooded the giant terracing.

The Welsh supporters were in a little group away up in the top corner and everywhere else the Scots had simply taken over. Don't get me wrong, I'm not criticizing the Welsh fans when I point out that they weren't there in the expected numbers. It was simple, really: our punters made up their minds that they *would* be there. They decided that they would all get tickets. I've never known them more determined, except maybe before the 1981 Wembley match when the English FA tried to ban them, and they went down to show that a ban couldn't work.

At Anfield, they had simply got it into their heads that this was where we would qualify and they intended to be there to see it. That's the way it worked out too.

The Welsh FA were criticized for taking the game to Anfield. But they would have been limited to 10,000 fans at Cardiff. What kind of trouble could that have produced? And would the criticism have been made if Alan Rough hadn't made that marvellous save from big Tosh when it seemed that the Welsh would score? I don't think so.

There was controversy too about the penalty which Don Masson scored from – but we did get another goal when I scored towards the end of the game to make it 2–0.

After the game I felt sorry for Tosh and Joey. Even

though it was such a great night for us I thought about them because they are every bit as patriotic as any of our lads could be. And Tosh had helped me a lot when I had joined up at Anfield just a couple of months before. Joey of course was just a great guy. So my thoughts were with them.

These feelings can come after games. They can't come before or during them. Then you have to go out and win for your country. Our victory over Wales was enough to take us to Argentina and that's what we owed ourselves. We felt we owed it also to those fans who had travelled south so hopefully and were now talking of Argentina as if it was just around the corner. The favourite direction given in Glasgow around that time was fairly simple and to the point, 'Take Laker to New York and then turn left.' A few brave souls did just that!

By now the hysteria was beginning to build and there were doubts beginning to prey on my mind. I think I had some instinctive worries because I wasn't used to Ally's style of managing. Ally MacLeod was a good inspirational manager – he had shown that with Aberdeen where he won the League Cup. And as he had done at Ayr and Aberdeen, he wanted to tell the world about his team. At club level that was part of his job, because he needed publicity for the provincial clubs he bossed. At international level he didn't need to do it so much. I'm a great believer in talking about something only when you've done the job. Looking back, I feel that he placed a lot of unnecessary pressure on the players when he talked of winning medals in Argentina. People began to believe that all we had to do was turn up. He didn't talk that way to us, incidentally. He didn't tell us that we would finish in the top four in the finals. That was for the public. A lot of things Ally said to the press he didn't say to us. It left me wondering, sometimes, what was going on. People think the manager speaks for the players and that isn't always right. Certainly it wasn't right then!

Initially he wanted to set up some kind of disciplinary system among the players. He had instituted something of the kind at Aberdeen and he wanted to introduce it to the Scottish squad. He was going to fine players who were late for meals, or for training, or for team talks. Stuff like that. I don't know what the fines were because I was never affected; I don't even know if anyone was ever fined, though wee Lou Macari was supposed to be fined at one time for being late. I think he wanted to show that he could be a strict disciplinarian, but I don't really remember anyone doing anything that warranted being fined.

He also used the kickoff tactic he had used at Aberdeen, in which most of the players line up on one side of the park at the kickoff. That was more a piece of showmanship than a specific tactical plan. At least, that's how I saw it.

It's funny to throw my mind back now to those eventful eighteen months. At the time it seemed that Ally dominated everything . . . from being the hero before we went to South America to being the scapegoat when we came home. Yet despite his being a larger-than-life character to the general public I don't have any great memories of his reign as Scotland's team boss. It's hard to recall anything special about his team talks. Difficult to say how well he motivated us. On the tour of South America the year before the World Cup and all its troubles he seemed fine. He told us what to expect in the three matches and we did all right. Sometimes, though, there didn't appear to be a lot of substance to the things he was saying. He didn't have as much information about them as other managers had had before him. Yet that was balanced by the fact that he wanted us to go out and play positively in most of our matches. I find it hard to reconcile all the sides of Ally MacLeod. I don't think back and say that he was great at one aspect of managing the team – but I don't look back and think he was hopeless either. It's all somewhere in between; he was a complex personality.

Whatever else he possessed or lacked, look at it how you will, he did have the power to weave dreams for the fans. They were on the march with 'Ally's army' all right . . . they believed him when he said medals were there to be won . . . and they went all the way to Argentina to see us do it. Ally was their messiah even when things started to go wrong in the home international championship before we left for Argentina. We didn't win a game in that competition, but the fans believed in him so much that thousands turned up at Hampden to give us a sendoff.

That was something else that made me uncomfortable. It's just not in my nature to take laps of honour before achieving anything and that's what that Hampden farewell was about. Mind you, the money taken at the gates did go to the Save Hampden fund. But for me it would have been enough to tell the people when we were travelling and they could have waved us off. Which was just what they did when we left for Prestwick and the jet which was to take us to Buenos Aires and then on to Cordoba where our headquarters for the section games were to be.

Still, although there were mistakes, Ally was a loyal manager. That was appreciated by the players. Perhaps it led him to make mistakes in his team selections or in the squad he took with him to South America. But there is a lot to be said for loyalty and he stayed with the men who had taken him through the vital qualification games – and had given him two victories in doing so.

7

The Argentina nightmare

We left for Argentina the way we had returned from West Germany four years earlier – with the fans waiting to cheer us, with bands playing and flags and banners waving. There was one essential difference – when we came back from West Germany we did so with heads high and at least with an unbeaten three games behind us.

Going to Argentina we had still done no more than qualify and there had already been signs at the training camp that the team spirit was not to be the same as it was on that first World Cup adventure. The results in the home internationals hadn't helped us any. Even though every game was at Hampden we couldn't register a single win. We drew with Northern Ireland 1–1, managed the same result against Wales and then lost to England 1–0 when Stevie Coppell scored the only goal of the game.

There had been off-field rumblings, too. Discussions about bonus payments had started at Dunblane Hydro where we stayed before the Hampden games. They had broken up with none of the players really happy at the way things were going. There were too many loose ends, too many things not properly explained to us. And so the seeds of dissension were sown in the camp. That kind of money squabble was the last thing we wanted. Or needed.

It was to be a long time before the bonus question was sorted out to everyone's satisfaction. Or, at least, close to everyone's satisfaction. It hung over the squad until

The 1974 Scotland World Cup team. Back row *(left to right)*: David Harvey, Jim Holton, Joe Jordan, Danny McGrain, John Blackley; front row *(left to right)*: Kenny Dalglish, Sandy Jardine, Peter Lorimer, Billy Bremner, Davie Hay, Denis Law. Three of this squad helped the team to Spain, 1982 – Joe, Danny and myself

The game against Zaire in the 1974 World Cup was tough. Defender Mwepu is poised over the fallen Denis Law who was saved by the intervention of the keeper, Kazadi

That agonizing moment
from the 1974 World
Cup when skipper Billy
Bremner missed from a
few yards against Cup-
holders Brazil

Willie Ormond, popular
and unassuming
Scotland manager,
helped me a lot during
my early days with the
international team

Controversial but dynamic. I believe that Tommy Docherty revitalized Scottish international football in his brief spell as team boss

That wonderful feeling – defeating Bruges at Wembley in 1978 gave me my first European Cup medal and, as an added bonus, I scored the winning goal

International team-mates in direct opposition. Manchester United's Martin Buchan closes in during the 1979 FA Cup semi-final at Maine Road

Bill Shankly, the man
who moulded the present
Liverpool team and
advised me never to lose
my Scottish accent –
which I haven't

Bob Paisley took over
from Shankly reluctantly,
but has done a
marvellous job

My first club boss and present international manager, Jock Stein *(left)* with Scotland's supremo in Argentina, Ally MacLeod

We salvaged some pride from the 1978 World Cup by beating Holland, eventual runners-up, 3-2. It would have been 4-2 if this goal had not been disallowed

The man I replaced at Anfield, England skipper Kevin Keegan – here being challenged by Northern Ireland skipper Martin O'Neill

Scotland v. Switzerland, European Championships March 1983. I'm brought down by Swiss defender Hermann in our match at Hampden Park

In action against Spanish champions Atletico Bilbao during the 1983
European Cup run which ended in a penalty-kick triumph in Rome

the day the SFA officials themselves stepped in to hammer out the understanding which should have been reached weeks earlier in Dunblane.

That was all in the background. As far as the public was concerned – and not only the Scottish public, but the world at large – Scotland were heading for Argentina to win a medal. That was the phrase Ally had used from the time the draw was made in Buenos Aires in January 1978. He repeated it time after time and so we flew out from Prestwick with five million people believing that we would be returning even more successful than we had been in West Germany.

It was a tall order. We had been placed in the same group as Holland, runners-up in 1974; Peru, who would be at home in the South American conditions; and Iran, who looked easy opposition on paper but did bring back memories of Zaire and the problems they had given us four years before.

We should have taken the first hint we had that things would not go smoothly and learned from it. We arrived in Cordoba, were welcomed at the airport by the local people and by our own advance guard from the tartan army and then headed for Alta Gracia, described to us as the Gleneagles of Argentina. That was to be our home for most of the time we were there. On the way, the bus broke down.

Maybe that was an omen. Just a hint of all the disasters which were to hit us over the two weeks or so that we were in Argentina. The bus breaking down was a minor worry . . . but later that night some of the lads went out for a walk in the hotel grounds and the first of the garbled stories was sent home.

That was to be something which plagued us all through our time in Argentina: stories being exaggerated either in

Argentina or back home in our own newspapers. This was
a typical example, an innocent stroll around the grounds
which turned into front-page news suggesting that the lads
involved had been in some kind of trouble. We'd arrived
at the hotel in Alta Gracia, had a meal and some of the
lads decided they would go for a stroll. I can't remember
the identities of all the lads who went out but Alan Rough
was there and Sandy Jardine was there. All they did was
ask Ally if they could take a walk down to the casino,
which was in the grounds of the hotel, and take a look
round . . . the way anyone does when they arrive at a
hotel where they have never been before. It wasn't late, in
fact, it was right after we had eaten. The lads just wanted
to stretch their legs, so Ally said OK. We hadn't had a
chance to see round the place when we arrived and on
their way back from the casino the lads thought they
would jump over a fence which had been built around the
buildings where the team was billeted.

If they had tried to go the long way round it would have
taken a while, and they just wanted to get back to the
hotel.

It seemed the obvious thing to do, with the hotel so
close on the other side of that fence. But one of the
security guards came along and stopped them. As we'd
just arrived, the guard didn't know who the lads were, and
naturally the language barrier didn't contribute anything
to the situation. Eventually some of the SFA officials saw
what was happening and the whole thing was straightened
out in a matter of minutes. Afterwards all of us had a good
laugh. Back home, though, the story grew somewhat. The
fence – just an ordinary fence it was – became electrified.
The fact that the guard was armed was highlighted –
though all the guards were armed as a matter of course. So
the lads' wives kicked off the World Cup believing that

their husbands had been close to death on the very first night. Yet in Alta Gracia we were looking on it as a laugh; that's all it was.

Later, when more and more stories started to drift back home, more sinister readings were placed on that first muddle. Gradually the pressures began to build. On the players and on the manager.

A picture was printed in an Argentinian football magazine showing two of our players, Asa Hartford and Sandy Jardine, sitting at the World Cup headquarters in Cordoba. They were sipping on a couple of Cokes and some of the girl assistants who worked there were asking for autographs. It was totally innocent – until you read the caption! This said that the players were in a Cordoba nightclub being entertained by the club hostesses. It was nonsense and everyone who had been in the Cordoba HQ knew that. We had gone there to get our accreditation passes, those vital pieces of plastic which allowed us into the training camps, into our own hotel and into the grounds. But while it was nonsense, it was dangerous nonsense when added to the stories which soon began to go the rounds. Predictably the stories began after we had lost the opening match. Suddenly, the hotel at Alta Gracia was reckoned to be the scene of wild parties and the little town itself – just a collection of shops and one or two cafes – was made out to be a South American version of Las Vegas.

None of it was true . . . but it went back home, sent by news reporters and the stories had the wives and families there under greater pressure than ever. I'd like to make it clear here that these stories were sent mainly by the newsmen as opposed to the sports writers. The journalists we deal with almost all the time, the people who write about football, weren't involved in the tales of excess which spilled out of Argentina and which were proved to be untrue in the end.

None of the stories helped us – but I'm not using them to excuse the performances we gave in the opening two games against Peru and Iran. Remember the stories did begin almost immediately on our arrival, with the mix-up at Alta Gracia when the lads tried to jump the fence.

We went into those opening two games blind. Ally hadn't gone to see either of the teams play and he wasn't able to tell us anything at all about them. That wasn't a great departure for him – Ally was never the kind of manager who dwelt too long on the opposing team. He preferred to lift players by concentrating on their own strengths, and convincing them that they were the best team going out onto that field. At the top level though, it's difficult when you don't know anything at all. We had been told that Peru were a team of ageing stars, remnants from their glory days in the Mexico tournament eight years earlier. Their inside forward Teofilio Cubillas was supposed to be 'tubby and overweight'. Everything we were told about them was negative.

When we scored early through Joe Jordan it was almost as if things were going to go according to the script Ally had written. The only thing wrong was that the Peruvians hadn't read Ally's version of things. They hit back and the 'tubby' Cubillas, who didn't look that much overweight to us when we saw him score, was one of their stars. They had a few, mind you. We had none. After Don Masson's penalty in the second half, they really got on top. It's wrong to say Don missed it, because their goalkeeper, a madcap called Quiroga who became one of the personalities of the tournament, saved it. In fact he saved it well.

I felt sorry for Don. His penalty at Anfield had helped us to get to Argentina and then a penalty being saved turned him into a villain in Cordoba. It wasn't as simple as that. Don took that penalty as well as he had taken the one at Anfield. The difference was that the keeper saved this one *and* at a time when the Peruvians were getting on top in the game. There's no doubt about that. Scoring early could have been a bad thing for us. Though it might sound silly to say so, that goal may have given us a false confidence. That made us forget about being cautious and we were caught out as a result.

That game was on the Saturday, after just over a week in Argentina, a week where things always seemed to be going wrong. There was the trouble over the training ground, for example. When Ally had visited Alta Gracia five months earlier he had looked at a local ground to train on because you were allowed at the stadium in Cordoba only on certain days. This one seemed ideal. It was being relaid when Ally was there and he had promises that it would be perfect for our arrival in June. It wasn't. In fact it was a disaster. It was rutted and uneven and in one of the early training games Joe Jordan damaged an ankle, which came close to keeping him out of that first match against Peru. It wasn't possible to work out properly there, and that didn't add much to confidence at the camp!

You couldn't blame Ally for the training-ground fiasco because promises had been made to him. We were left wondering if the Brazilians or West Germans would have the same problems . . .

The hotel, too, wasn't exactly Gleneagles. It had a nice setting, huge grounds around it and marvellous views. Because of the security though, we were left with little chance to do anything and once we had taken the few minutes needed to stroll round the village of Alta Gracia, there was nothing left to see. So there wasn't a lot of chance to relax away from the oppressive feeling surrounding the training camp. Basically, I don't think that our players are too good at being cooped up in a training camp for too long a spell. They can't accustom themselves to a routine the way Italian or South American players seem to be able to. Which is why our clubs don't take their players away for long spells at a time the way they do in other countries.

Another blow fell after that Peru game. As is usual in World Cup games, two of the players were taken for dope tests. Officials draw lots to decide which players from each team should go. This time my name came out along with that of Willie Johnston. Off we went, had the tests, and returned to the dressing room. It all seemed routine, especially to me, because I'd had to go through it before. This time though, the roof fell in on us. The front-page stories which went home *were* correct – Willie Johnston's dope test proved positive! The news reached the players late on the Sunday night while Sports Minister Denis Howell was at a reception at our hotel.

Bud – that's Willie Johnston's nickname – had taken a tablet called Reactivan. He had been given the tablets by his club doctor at West Bromwich Albion and he had brought them with him to Argentina. In spite of the warnings the team doctor gave us about drugs which were banned, Bud had taken the tablet and hadn't told the doctor about it. The tablet contained some amount of a banned drug and so Willie Johnston and the team were in disgrace. Not to mention a total state of shock.

I felt sorry for the doctor, Dr John Fitzsimons, who had also been my club doctor at Celtic Park. He had done everything he could possibly do. He had warned us about the various drugs which were banned, and he had asked us if we had any tablets of any kind with us. No one had admitted to having any. Still, the wee doc took the whole thing very personally. We all felt bad about that. And none of us were too happy at the way wee Bud was treated at the end either. OK, he had made a mistake, he had been wrong to do what he did. But then he was whisked out of the hotel in a car, driven to Buenos Aires overnight and then packed onto a plane back to Britain. In disgrace. We the players thought someone might have gone with him at least. Still, the SFA had acted before FIFA could impose any ban on the team. They had banned Willie Johnston for life and they wanted him away from the squad before the publicity worsened.

The drug charge would have cost us the two points against Peru whether or not we had been able to win. We prepared for the match against little Iran in an atmosphere which seemed to be worsening by the hour. That game, those ninety minutes against the Iranians, the least known of any of the teams in the finals, were without doubt the worst minutes of my whole career. Nothing before and nothing since has plunged me to the depths the way that game did. We had to win to give ourselves a chance of qualifying and to regain some of the respect we had lost in that sickening opener against Peru. It didn't turn out that way. Quite simply, the nightmare continued with barely a pause.

We didn't lose the game, but all we could manage was a 1–1 draw and our goal was scored by one of their players, their captain Eskandarian. It was a dreadful night for us and for the fans. To make matters worse, the own goal gave us the lead, and then we gave away a goal. It was a game we would have won nine times out of ten but in those circumstances, in Argentina, it was always on the cards that we might lose something. And when we left the field the tartan army booed and jeered us. When we left the stadium they stayed behind to jeer the team bus, to burn their lion-rampant flags, to give us as much stick as they could. It was terrible but I couldn't blame them for turning on us. Scots people like fighters, but in that game we didn't even fight. We were terrible. I felt sorry for these fans because we had let them down.

I think all of us who played in that game still carry scars on our memory that even the revival against Holland couldn't completely heal. By then we had moved down to Mendoza and a change of hotel helped lift us. Strangely, the players also began to work together better; it was like 1974. Things had gone so badly now that we simply had to get together and get a result. We had to do it for ourselves and we had to do it for these fans. Some of them had spent their life-savings getting there, and we hadn't given them anything to remember. Nothing good, at any rate . . .

Holland were the favourites in our section, the European team most strongly tipped in the tournament. At last it came right. We liked the playing surface at the Mendoza stadium. It was softer and lusher than the one in Cordoba and it suited our style better. The lads fought superbly and played so much better than we had played in the other games. We won 3–2 and little Archie Gemmill scored one of the finest goals of the entire tournament. We didn't qualify because we had lost three points before going into that one, but it was something which helped save our faces a little . . . although what had happened before probably meant that we couldn't properly save anything. I know that's the way I felt, but we did leave the fans with one good memory.

Our return was all so different from that after West Germany. Then we flew into Glasgow with crowds waiting to cheer us. This time I was happy to leave the main party at Gatwick and get home to Liverpool and my family.

I think every one of us knew that we had let people

down by the performances in those two matches. Not just ourselves. Not just the fans who had trekked all those thousands of miles to support us. Every single Scot was let down, everyone in the country and the exiles abroad. All the Scots who had dreams of us going to Argentina and doing well. The whole country had been disappointed and we realized that. It took a long time for the hurt to wear away . . .

8

Diary of disaster

I still don't know why I did it. It's not something that I usually do, but during our two weeks in Argentina I took notes every day of what was happening. Just short notes, jottings if you like, but enough to keep those disastrous weeks fresh still in my mind.

I have already described some of the horror of Argentina, but when I look back at my diary more and more detail floods back to me. That's why I am reproducing parts of the diary here and recalling in detail some of the private hell we went through as players . . .

THURSDAY – training at stadium. Team talk, five minutes. Not really helpful.

That was a couple of days before the game and by then we knew that training at the stadium was going to be best for us. The local ground was a disaster area. I remember it was a good workout, but the talk about the game literally lasted five minutes. Ally really didn't tell us anything about Peru. Mind you, he hadn't seen them so it wasn't easy for him to give any detailed rundown on their players or their style of play. He could not even tell us any of the set-pieces which they tried to work.

SATURDAY – long lie. Pre-match departure 2.45 P.M. Kickoff 4.45 P.M. No team talk. No geeing up. Lost 3–1. No team changes.

It was a strange dressing-room setup at the Cordoba

stadium. The room was split into two and that's just about the way the team was splitting up as well. Half the players were in one side and the rest in the other; at half time, instead of getting us together Ally left things as they were. The game wasn't beyond us by then. We were drawing 1–1 but they had started to come through in droves from the midfield. The way things were in the dressing room didn't help us sort things out. We had the defence blaming the forwards and the forwards blaming the defence and out of all the talking nothing concrete came up. In an effort to get the team back in control of the match, I thought Ally should have called all of us round him and tried to work things out. Instead things seemed simply to get worse. It was the first time I'd noticed a lack of leadership and it was a time when we needed leadership badly.

SUNDAY – press conference. No blame whatever. Eight players off form. 'Too many cliques' – manager.

The team manager had held a press conference in the morning and this is what he was supposed to have said. There was a fair bit of resentment among the players and although Ally denied saying it eventually, we felt a little bit let down. If you are in something together then you have to stick together. Not just when things are going well, but when they are going badly too. More especially when they are going badly.

He was also quoted as referring to 'cliques' among the players. Perhaps he was right about that. There were cliques in the squad, more so than there were in West Germany, and when that happens, the whole team suffers. It can happen very easily. Someone said to me recently that players are guilty of talking behind other players' backs. What he meant was that when players get together to talk things over they are reluctant to say openly to another player anything about a specific match situation in which he had been involved. They say it when the player isn't there, but it would be better if it was done face to face. Not so that they fall out but just to get things straightened out. Maybe that's the kind of thing Ally meant.

There's no doubt, though, that some of the players were angry at having all the blame attached to them. The cracks were starting to show.

MONDAY – trained at Alta Gracia. Wee WJ sent home. Drive to BA arranged. Meet with WH tomorrow at 12.00.

The Willie Johnston affair had broken the night before and he was whisked out of the camp and driven all the way to Buenos Aires. That didn't help improve the mood in the hotel. Nor did the meeting I mention – WH being the SF president Willie Harkness. Trouble had blown up over the bonuses which had been worked out by the SFA and spelled out to Ally. The trouble was that Ally hadn't given the players the full details!

TUESDAY – trained Cordoba. Met WH. No more money but I felt good meeting. Manager tells press the team. GS hears from his folks.

It was a mixed day, that one. The meeting with Willie Harkness was good. The SFA are often criticized but honestly they did their best for the squad. There was no way that everything could be sorted out exactly how some of the players wanted, but Willie Harkness and his vice-president, Tommy Younger, took the time to speak to us and explained the whole situation. As far as they had known, it had all been dealt with at Dunblane during the home international championship. They thought that Ally had told us all the details and that we had agreed to their proposals. I felt better after the meeting. It had cleared the air around one of the problems . . .

Then the other arose. The press were told who would be in the team to play Iran, but the players were left in the dark. When GS – Graeme Souness – phoned home he found out from his parents that he was not playing. Graeme had been given a strong hint that he was going to be in the side for that second match, so he was unhappy, obviously. Actually, all of us were unhappy. I think it's wrong that the press should be told the team before the players have been told. The player has to go out there and do a job so he's entitled to know if he's playing or not before anyone outside the squad knows. It was another action which brought resentment out among the players. I think Ally should have told us. And he should have realized that the lads were phoning home regularly and that someone would learn that the team had been named.

WEDNESDAY – up for tea and toast. Team talk at 12.30. MS dossier never mentioned, nor AR's. My fifty-sixth cap. Left 2.45. 1–1, another disaster. Press stake out Alta Gracia.

MS was the Welsh team manager, Mike Smith, who apparently had supplied Ally with information on the Iranian team. Wales had gone out to Teheran to play them a few months earlier and beaten them 1–0. AR was the Scottish national coach Andy Roxburgh, who had gone to watch Iran in their first match against Holland. While Ally obviously had their information on Iran available he never gave any of it to us. OK, so we should be able just to go out there and beat Iran, but it's helpful to know something about them: to know about their set pieces, if they do anything special at free kicks or corners, and just generally how they play. We didn't get anything like that at the team talk. The game was a disaster, the worst I've known, and the press were back at the hotel to see if there was any trouble. By then they wanted blood. But there was little chance of them getting any stories of trouble. We were scarcely off the camp.

Really, a lot of the stories about the squad came about because the supporters were going around in Cordoba wearing Scotland jerseys, some of them with players' names on them, and signing autographs. The Argentinians thought they *were* players. They really did think that we were hanging around the bars in Cordoba instead of being at our hotel. That led to a lot of the bother we had to put up with.

THURSDAY – long lie. Get Tunisia strip. Train 3.30. No manager to be seen. Hear DM sold his story to *News of the World* for Sunday.

The Tunisian team arrived at our hotel and one of their players gave me a strip to bring back home. It was a bad day at the hotel. We didn't see Ally at all; by this time the pressures had reached him too. His wife was apparently being hounded by the press at home and things were just too much for him. I think everyone remembers those television pictures of him in the dugout at the Iran game. We were left to muddle through ourselves. There was a real lack of leadership by now and there was no one around who could take over from Ally while he was having his own troubles. I could understand what he was going through. His wife was having problems back home, his world had collapsed around him in Alta Gracia and that day, a rest day for the team, he just wanted to be on his own. A few of us felt the same way.

DM was Don Masson. When Willie Johnston was in trouble Don had gone to the team manager and said that he had also taken the same pills which had shown up in the dope test. Don was sharing a room with Willie Johnston and I think he thought he might be able to lessen the punishment for his roommate. He hadn't taken the pills of course, but he did sell a story to the *News of the World* about the whole affair. I was disappointed in Don for that. We were all under pressure and we didn't need one of the squad adding needlessly to it. It was his decision, of course, but I don't think it was in the best interests of the rest of us; nor do I think he should have done it. There seemed no end to the problems, which were coming fast on top of each other.

FRIDAY – training 2.00 at Cordoba. Private. Best session we've had.

Things had gone so badly that we realized we simply had to pull together to get the improvement we needed before that last game against Holland. There was so much more purpose about the training session. All of us, without any deep discussion, seemed to realize that we simply *had* to get things right. We were all in trouble and so we had to pick ourselves up and get on with the job. It was a bit like the team effort in 1974 after the troubles in Largs and Norway when everyone buckled down and worked for the good of the squad and forgot individual priorities. If only it had started that way. I think I had the first feelings then that things would go well against the Dutch the following Sunday. It was not only me – I think that most of the lads

realized that we had to get out there and do something
rather special.

SATURDAY – leave for Mendoza. No training. Individual team talk.

There was a sense of relief at getting away from Alta
Gracia and that helped us all, I think. The team talk was
better too and we were more familiar with the Dutch style
and with their players. We knew what we had to do in this
one.

SUNDAY – Holland 3–2. Reception, Plaza Hotel. Bruce
Millan.

The Scottish Secretary of State Bruce Millan was at a
special reception for us in the Plaza Hotel and at last we
were able to win a victory. None of us felt like celebrating
– we were out of the tournament. Mind you, that one
good result simply underlined how badly we had played in
the other two matches.

In fact we had come close to qualifying. Another goal
would have been enough to take us into the next round of
the tournament.

It had been so different from the beginning of that
game. We had played as a team, as we should have done
right from the start. There was a snap about our play
which caught the Dutch by surprise. In an opening spell
Joe Jordan hit the bar and I had a goal disallowed as the
Dutch defended desperately.

Then it seemed as if it would all turn sour for us again.
In thirty-four minutes the referee awarded them a penalty
and Rob Rensenbrink scored – the one thousandth goal of
the World Cup competition and it looked as if it would
beat us.

But that day we seemed able to draw on extra reserves and a minute before half time I levelled the scores. Three minutes after half time we were awarded a penalty ourselves, Archie Gemmill scored and for the first time since that opening half hour against Peru, our fans were behind us once more. It was great to hear them and they almost brought the stadium roof in when in sixty-eight minutes wee Archie scored the best goal of the competition. Incidentally, that's not my description, though of course I agree. The goal was described that way in the official FIFA report on all the games played in Argentina.

The joy lasted a couple of minutes before Johnny Rep scored their second with a long range drive. But before the end we hit the woodwork again and at last we showed the form which had carried us through the qualifying games and across the world to Argentina. It was some consolation.

TUESDAY – leave for Buenos Aires. Flight delayed. Arrive 4.00 P.M. Players refuse to stay in hotel which has been booked. Transfer to Sheraton.

Even at the end there was a muddle. We were booked into a poor standard hotel and had to get the SFA to change the booking. They did and we prepared to return home in some comfort.

WEDNESDAY – leave to come home. Flight's on time and I get to Manchester at 6.15 P.M.

The nightmare was over.

Or maybe it won't ever be over. We got home just under three weeks after we had flown out from Scotland with the cheers ringing in our ears. Even now it seems that the stay in Argentina was so much longer. So many things happened to us over there . . . and so few of them were good. There were players who were never to play again for their country, some because of the form they had shown, some because of disciplinary measures taken against them. There were three of the latter – Willie Johnston banned over his dope test and Don Masson and my old Celtic Park team-mate Lou Macari because of newspapers articles they wrote at the time.

It was an ill-fated expedition. I'd never like to go through anything quite as bad as that again and I hope that as players we never let down the Scottish people the way we did by our results in those two opening matches. The displays then were unforgivable.

9

That first European Cup – at last

I think that growing up in the shadow of the Lisbon Lions when I was a youngster at Celtic Park always made the European Cup that little bit special for me.

Always that was the glittering prize to aim for. The Celtic team of 1967 had done it and made themselves a little bit of history. They were the first British team to win the cup and they remain the only team to have done so with players of one nationality only. So around Celtic Park when I signed and when I eventually made my breakthrough into the first team the thought of emulating that Lisbon team was always with us. Somehow though, we never did manage to do it. We came close, with two semifinal appearances, one against Inter Milan when we failed on penalty kicks at Celtic Park. The other was the dreadful match against Atletico Madrid where they had four players ordered off at Celtic Park. That was without any doubt the worst game I've ever played in as far as violence is concerned. I think if they had had one more player sent off then the referee would have abandoned the game and we would have been awarded the tie. It wouldn't have been very satisfactory, I suppose, but it would have carried us into the final instead of them.

So it was disappointment all the time for me at Celtic. Liverpool though, who had established a powerful reputation for themselves on the Continent in the process, had won the trophy in Rome a few months before I went to Anfield. It was the trophy I'd dreamed about for ten years and the lure of European success was an important factor in my making the move to Liverpool in 1977. Obviously my hope was that we could go on and do it again with me in the side.

Yet in the second round of the next season's competition, we came close to being put out by the East German team Dynamo Dresden. If you look back at the records you won't believe that, but I can assure you that it is perfectly true; any of the lads at the park will tell you the same. It certainly didn't seem as if it would be that way when we played them at Anfield in the first leg. We'd been given a bye in the first round that year, so that match against Dresden was my first European game for Liverpool. We won it 5–1 with just under 40,000 fans there. It was a marvellous night. I remember big Tosh was playing and he flicked a header on for Alan Hansen to get the opening goal for us. Then it was a procession, with Jimmy Case getting two, Phil Neal one and Ray Kennedy the other. A fellow called Hafner scored for Dresden but it was a night to celebrate and I felt marvellous. This was the kind of European win I'd been hoping for and all the dreams began to take shape . . .

Yet in Dresden these same dreams almost fell apart again. They played superbly against us. Probably as well as any team I can remember facing in a European tie and I've played dozens of them down through the years. It's hard to believe that you could be in danger of losing a four-goal lead – but we were!

It became clear from the start that the East Germans were a far better team than they had seemed at Anfield. Maybe they froze there – Anfield does have that effect on teams. They were absolutely brilliant. I could see that we were, in fact, in danger of losing that lead. Clem (Ray Clemence) was magnificent. He kept us in the game. No kidding. He stopped them on his own for a spell when they were really buzzing. They scored two goals right after half time and we were in trouble. They needed just two more goals and that was us out of the tournament because of the away goal they had scored at Anfield. Then we went up the park and the ball was played high into their goal mouth. I went up with their goalkeeper and he dropped the ball and Stevie Heighway followed up, got to the ball and hit it in. That killed them off. They collapsed – but it was a long, long night.

I don't think that I've ever taken anything for granted in European football since that night. I don't believe that you can. Teams change tremendously when they are at home in front of their own crowds and I don't know any British teams who enjoy travelling behind the Iron Curtain. The food is always a problem, even though we often have our own with us, and there is just nothing to do. It becomes boring and that doesn't help anyone preparing for an important match.

That's not making excuses for that game, nor is it trying to take anything away from how Dynamo Dresden played. It was their night and they played marvellous football until Stevie scored. It's just one of the facts of football life in Europe . . .

The next round was the quarterfinals and we were drawn against the Portuguese champions Benfica, with the first leg away from home. There were 70,000 people in the Estadio de Luz that night and we went a goal behind when one of their international players – most of them were international players – Nene, scored. But Jimmy Case equalized. It was lashing rain that night and when Jimmy hit a low shot it skidded along the turf and went under the goalkeeper's body. Then Emlyn Hughes got the winner. He says he meant to score – I doubt that, and we kidded him about it. Still, he hit a ball from away out on the touchline and the wee goalkeeper, Bento, just couldn't reach it at all. It sailed over his head and went into the goal at the far post.

That was a great win for us and a very important one. When they came to Anfield we destroyed them and the crowd was close to 50,000 for that match. I won't forget that one because I scored my first ever European goal for the club. Their goalkeeper, Bento, had a nightmare match – yet a few years later he defied Scotland at Hampden. The first goal was a joke. Ian Callaghan shot and the wee man, Bento, tried to kick the ball clear with his left foot. It hit his right foot and ended up behind him in the net. It was unbelievable. But it counted and we were on our way to a solid win.

Then I scored my goal. I can still remember it. I got the ball in the inside-right position and hit the ball across goal, right past Bento and in at the far corner. It was a great feeling. They got one back, that man Nene again, but before the end Terry McDermott and Phil Neal had made it four and we were through to the semifinals with six goals over the two legs. By now the European dreams I had were coming closer and closer to reality.

Then came the semifinal draw, which paired Liverpool with our old rivals Borussia Moenchengladbach, the team the lads had beaten in Rome the previous season in the final. It was obviously going to be a difficult game and Borussia wanted revenge for the year before. They had a few right good players: Bertie Vogts, Rainer Bonhof, Jupp Heynckes – this was not going to be easy!

Strangely, Liverpool seemed to have the Indian sign on them. They were terrified, particularly about coming to Anfield. They seemed to have a massive inferiority complex, probably stemming from the defeat the year before. It was hard to grasp that a team with so much experience and so many big-name players should be afraid of us. That's how it was, though, even though they were able to beat us 2–1 in the first leg, which we played in the World Cup stadium in Düsseldorf. They took the lead through Hannes and then Davie Johnson nicked one back for us with a header. He'd come on as a sub and it was a good goal he scored.

That far-post goal had us level until the last two minutes of the match, when they were given a free kick about twenty-five yards out. Their dead-ball expert Rainer Bonhof stepped up to take it. I'll never forget it. It was the strangest free kick goal I think I've ever seen. We had the wall lined up OK and then he blasted it for goal. Clem had the ball covered all the way and then suddenly it seemed to rise. Clem had been behind it all the way, he had done everything right and then this happened. It didn't seem to spin and it didn't bend the way the one did when Bonhof scored against England. It just took a freakish rise up in the air. Clem tried to get to it but it was impossible. He was blamed afterwards in the press but I would never have blamed him at all. It was an astonishing goal and I've never seen a ball behave like that either before or since. It was a freak. That goal left us a goal down – though we did have the return at Anfield and we did realize by now that the Germans didn't relish the idea of coming to play us on our ground.

We won easily in the end and I scored again. Ray Kennedy had put us in front to start with then I scored and at half time we were two goals up. Then Jimmy Case hammered in the third. It was a no-contest really and so there I was, at last, in the final of the European Cup. And just to make things a little better for us the game was set to be played at Wembley. It was like a home game for most of the lads. We'd almost all played there at one time or another and it was a bit of a bonus knowing that we only had to travel down to London instead of heading into Europe again.

The team we were playing was the unfashionable Belgian champions Bruges, who had been guided through the earlier rounds by their coach Ernst Happel. They seemed frightened to death too. They came to Wembley prepared only to play defensively. They just sat back and hoped that they might catch us on the break. I suppose they thought that we had the experience on our side of playing in a final before. I suppose too that they must have worried at travelling to England to play the game where we were clearly tipped as favourites. We had an advantage, I suppose, but in a final that kind of advantage can place extra pressure on a team. People expect more from players. They think that you can simply go out there and lift the trophy without any real problems. That's never the case – especially when you are talking about the European Cup. So it wasn't easy – and it wasn't much of a spectacle for the 92,000 supporters either, I don't suppose. We were the only team who wanted to play. We won and that winner's medal I wanted so much was mine at last. I scored the goal too and that was a little extra for me to remember. The ball was played in to the near post initially and I got it there and hooked it over my head. I didn't see if anyone was there but usually someone like big Ray Kennedy is hanging about at the far post. Anyhow they got it and played it out and we all came out with them. Then Graeme Souness won a tackle and pushed the ball back into their box and I moved on to it.

Earlier the goalkeeper had come out to block a shot from Terry McDermott when he was going through the middle. So this time I waited until the keeper had committed himself and then when he had come out I lifted the ball over his body and it rolled into the net. That was it. That goal won the game. I suppose the way Bruges approached the match, it might always have been a question of just one goal doing it. Certainly they never had us under any pressure. Our only worry was that we would be caught out by a quick breakaway – it was the only tactic they used which might have given us any trouble at all. On the night though, it didn't work.

So three Scots were able to pick up medals that night: myself, Alan Hansen and Graeme Souness. Graeme had joined us in January from Middlesbrough and he had not been eligible to play in the quarterfinal against Benfica. He had to sit in the stand and watch that one. By the time the semifinals came around he was eligible and he came on as a substitute against Borussia in West Germany and then played for the whole game against them in the second leg at Anfield. Then, of course, he set up that goal for me in the final.

It was a great feeling to get that medal. One of the very best moments of my career. I'd moved on from Celtic searching for the success which would bring me a winner's medal in the European Cup and here it was inside one season. It was fairytale stuff – amd I loved it.

10

The Forest jinx, the Russian connection and another European win

From that high point we went into two years of troubles at European level. For most teams it's enough to qualify for the European Cup. Liverpool, just like Celtic, needed more than that. So to crash out of the tournament we had dominated for two years in the first round was difficult for all of us to swallow.

Twice it happened. Once to Nottingham Forest, who were labelled our jinx team, and once to the Russians from Dynamo Tbilisi.

Funnily enough Forest were a team who gave us problems, and I still don't understand why. Most of the times we played them we looked the better side. Yet they seemed able to steal the result they wanted whether it was a win or a draw. The results will tell you that they were a bogey side to us – but I don't think any one of us felt consciously afraid of them. It probably made us want to do better against them. It might have given us an extra push to get the result we wanted – but we always seemed to end up without a shred of luck when we played them.

That seemed true in other competitions quite apart from the European Cup tie – the game of the century they called it in England with us as holders and Forest as champions clashing in the number one competition. That match apart I can remember two typical games between us. One in midweek, a semifinal of the League Cup, one three days later in the English Cup.

In the first one we were all over them. We played them off the park; then in the last minute they got a penalty and John Robertson – my Scotland mate – scored and as it

turned out that was us out. We drew the second leg at
Anfield 1–1. On the Saturday we went back to the City
ground and Davie Johnson went through and hit a great
shot. It beat Peter Shilton, then came back off the post. I
can remember thinking, 'Here we go again,' and I know
that same thought went through the minds of the other
players as well. But for once the luck changed. Shilton
dropped the ball right at my feet and I scored. We went on
to win that one 2–0.

The European tie was something else. Cloughie (Nottingham Forest manager Brian Clough) did his usual
talking before the game about how his team, novices in
Europe, had no chance against us; we were the champions; we were the team with the European pedigree; we
were the team he hadn't wanted to play against. It was all
there, Cloughie trying to con us. He didn't succeed. He
might have conned the punters a little bit but he wasn't
able to do that to us. We had heard it all before from
managers right across Europe and we weren't likely to fall
for it. But we did make a mistake, a vital mistake, a
mistake which we would not have made if we had been
playing against one of the top teams from Europe.

All of us know what we did wrong and I'd like to think
that it won't happen again but I wouldn't guarantee it
because old habits die hard. This is what happened in that
match . . .

We went to the City ground to play a team we have to
face two or three times a season in the League or in Cup
games . . . a team which is familiar to us in a situation
which is also familiar to us. That was where we made our
mistake. When Forest went a goal ahead we reacted in
exactly the way we would have reacted in a normal
English First Division match. We didn't drop back and
play patiently. We didn't push the ball around and keep
possession the way we would have done in Lisbon or

Madrid or Dresden or Munich. Instead we went looking for an equalizer. We chased a goal just the way we would have done in a League game, and so near the end Colin Barrett scored a second goal for them and that was us in trouble. When they came to Anfield a couple of weeks later for the return *they* didn't make that mistake. They put up the shutters and we couldn't break down their defence. So we were out.

It was hard to take, especially when all of us realized our error. The following season we came up against Dynamo Tbilisi and I wouldn't make excuses. We lost to a good side, a very good side, and it showed that Russia was emerging as a powerful force in world football once more after so many years in the wilderness. The way the Russians performed in their World Cup qualifying games which followed our match showed that. They had good players. It's always a bit easier to take defeat when you can see that and acknowledge it. Not that we liked it any more.

When we qualified again the next year we were determined to prove that we were not the spent force that people were making us out to be. And we succeeded even more than I had hoped . . .

The great thing about that 1980 campaign was the number of good goals we were able to score and the number of good performances we were able to provide. OK, it started off with an easy touch, the Finnish champions Oulou Pallosseoura, nobody could pronounce it but that didn't worry us. It was, on paper, a tie we should win, though it really doesn't matter to me whether we get a hard tie or an easy one in the early rounds of the tournament. I know there is a school of thought which suggests an easy game to start with helps to build you towards the bigger things which must come eventually. My own view is simple – if you are going to win then you're going to have to beat the good teams some time or another so if it's early then let it be early. It doesn't worry me.

After all, any tie at all can provide its own difficulties. We had some problems over there because the pitch was bad and we could only manage a 1–1 draw. Terry McDermott scored and then they equalized near the end. But at Anfield we turned it on. There were some great goals that night! It was one of those nights when everything went right for us and we scored ten. Graeme Souness got three, Terry Mac (Terry McDermott) scored another hat trick, David Fairclough had a couple and Sammy Lee and Ray Kennedy finished it all off. What a good night that was for the punters. And it set the pattern for most of the displays we gave that year.

In the next round we were drawn against Aberdeen. That was a game which worried me beforehand, because I knew that once the Scotland v. England angle was brought into play the Aberdeen lads would play out of their skins.

They were a good side, Aberdeen, and they proved that the next year. They took on Ipswich and knocked them out of the UEFA Cup just a few months after the Ipswich lads had won that trophy. We played well up there in our tie; we won and Terry McDermott scored a great goal, another of those special goals that tournament produced for us. OK, it might have had a wee element of luck, it could have finished up off target . . . but it didn't. It was one Terry will always remember, I'm sure. That apart, we could have had a couple more. Jim Leighton, their keeper, had some good saves. So that was us 1–0 up. Then they came down to Liverpool and they attacked us at the start. Before we scored, Mark McGhee had a really good and dangerous run and Ray Clemence did well to stop him scoring – that would have made it all the harder for us. But a few minutes after that we got a corner and when the ball came over, poor Willie Miller tried to clear it and sliced it past his own keeper. From then on we controlled things. There was only one team in it after that. Phil Neal scored, I scored and Alan Hansen scored another of those specials. He went through on his own to tuck it away. That was the Aberdeen challenge finished and we were left looking forward to the quarterfinals, which would take place the following spring.

As our gaffer, Bob Paisley, always says, the great thing about getting through that second round is knowing that you have so much to look forward to as the season reaches a climax. The quarterfinals are something extra for the players and for the fans.

We were drawn against CSKA Sofia from Bulgaria with the first leg at Anfield. That was Graeme Souness's night. He had another hat trick – his second of the tournament – and you wouldn't see three better goals in a game. The first was between him and the goalie and he stuck it away from the 18-yards line. The others were tremendous shots – one in the top right-hand corner, one in the top left-hand corner. With Sammy Lee and Terry McDermott scoring as well it was a five-goal win. Behind the Iron Curtain, they had a bit of a flurry but that was all. Wee Sammy Lee hit a shot which struck the post and Davie Johnson, following up, tucked it away and we cruised into the last four without any problems at all. It had come a whole lot easier than I or anyone else at the club had expected. But the next game was destined to be different and harder.

Bayern Munich were the opposition and they were convinced that they would be able to halt us as we marched towards that final in Paris in May. It was the most difficult game we had to play and we didn't do too well at home. We could only draw 0–0, a result which delighted the West Germans and particularly their skipper Paul Breitner.

It was Breitner who made the biggest mistake of anyone in the tie. Not on the field but off the field, when after that first leg he started to shoot his mouth off about Liverpool. He called us 'unimaginative' and said that British football was short on ideas, that we were 'predictable' and that we would not now reach the final. I thought it was more than a bit unimaginative of him to do that. All it did was make us more determined than ever to do well. OK, Breitner did play well against us at Anfield. He looked a very good midfield player indeed, but sometimes it's easier to play in these ties away from home in midfield because you are asked to do less, constructively. You have to work hard, but basically you are in a situation where you are trying to hold things together, not necessarily trying to create anything. If you can create something then it's a bonus. He wasn't so good when it counted, in the next match. Just before the kickoff in the Olympic stadium in Munich the gaffer called wee Sammy Lee aside and told him that he had to pick up Breitner. It was his job to harry him and see how imaginative he could be. It worked well for us. Breitner didn't do anything in that second match and it proved to me again that no one should start shouting the odds in the game of football. It has a habit of rebounding on you, just as it rebounded on him that night. Ray Kennedy scored for us late on and it was only at the death that they were able to get an equalizer. Karl Heinz Rummenigge, Europe's Player of the Year, was the man who scored it but that one goal wasn't enough. With the away-goals rule counting in our favour we were through to another final – a date in Paris with Real Madrid.

My worry, though, was that I might miss that game. I took a bad knock against Bayern. Del Haye came in very late, he whacked me and I was in trouble. It was a bad injury and I didn't play again until the final. It was a case of treatment and training to get myself ready. There was no way that I wanted to miss the chance of winning another medal and I believed, like the rest of the lads, that we could do it all over again. It was an agonizing six weeks for me on the run up to the final, because the fear was always there that I might not make it. But once I was through fitness tests and had proved to the gaffer that I was ready and able to play, then the worries disappeared. All that counted was the game itself.

It was another hard game. Real Madrid are always a team who will attract neutral support because of their tradition. We knew too that they had been semifinalists the season before and that under their Yugoslav coach Vujadin Boskov they would be a hard team to beat. It wasn't a great game in the end. Not the kind of classic that people want to see. In a way it was a little bit like the other final I had played in at Wembley.

I think that teams don't want to risk too much in these games. Players don't want to hurl themselves forward and then lose a silly goal and maybe lose the cup because of that. It's about patience. All right, teams get criticized, but I don't think the Liverpool supporters would criticize us. We did take home that European Cup for them and that's their main concern. It's also the main concern of the players.

In a way that kind of match requires an early goal. Then the team which has gone behind must come back and the cat-and-mouse thing is over. The main thing that night was that we got the goal and Alan Kennedy scored it. It was a marvellous shot worthy of winning any major tournament and after it we had a couple more chances. We could have won a bit more easily in the end because the goal changed the game that little bit. They had to come out more and chase for a goal and we found the odd gap or two. They were committed a wee bit more. If that goal had come earlier, it might have been a better game.

Really, it's like a game of chess when you are playing at that level. You just can't give anything away. It was no use playing the way we had played against Forest and being the better team and losing. It's no use being beaten 4–0 and claiming that you were the best team. I would have loved the two finals to have been classics. It would have been great to have taken part in finals that even neutrals would remember happily. But it didn't work out that way. For our fans and our players, though, and for me personally, they were great finals because we won. In fact, the winning of that first European Cup medal was probably the best night of my footballing life.

I remember scoring the goal that night and I ran off the field and hurdled the advertising boards to wave to our punters. They've been so good to me and I'll never forget that moment. They took to me from that first Charity Shield game and I've always been grateful to them for the backing they have given me in all the years I've been with the club.

Looking back at all the teams we've played in Europe, Dynamo Dresden are the best I've come up against. They had a sweeper called Dorner and he kept hitting these sixty- and seventy-yard passes to the wingers which really tore us apart. That's the second leg I'm talking about, mind you. They were magnificent in that match . . . yet it's a team probably no one will remember. They'll be forgotten while the Real Madrids and Benficas and Bayerns are talked about so much more. Yet for ninety minutes they were the best team I've ever been asked to face.

11

I'm a Scot – not an Anglo!

If there is any one word in football which offends me then
it is the term used to describe the Scottish international
players who play in England. 'Anglos' they call us. And I
hate it!

I am as Scottish as anyone and when people make
distinctions against me, and I'm sure all the other players
feel much the same way, then I get angry. Why should you
be termed an Anglo simply because you happen to earn
your living south of Gretna? We feel as strongly about our
country as any of the lads playing at home do. I didn't
change any just because Celtic happened to sell me to
Liverpool. That move didn't alter overnight my outlook
on playing for my country.

In fact, there are times when you feel even more
intensely patriotic when you are living away from Scotland. I'm not just putting my own attitude forward here,
I'm thinking of all the exiles I've met when I've been
abroad with the national team, or with Celtic or
Liverpool. These exiles are desperate to have any
memento of home. Playing in England, too, we often have
to put up with a lot of stick from the other players if we
have done badly. That helps to make you more conscious
of your country.

The tag has been with us a long, long time. But as far as
I'm concerned it's a false one which I wish could be
dropped. I've been able to see the question from both
sides: first as an established international with Celtic and
now as one of the senior professionals in the Scotland
side, but playing with Liverpool.

I mentioned earlier that when I first broke into the Scotland team I was in awe of the bigger name players. It wasn't anything they said or did which made me feel that way. It was my own stupidity, if you like. I used to think that they might be wondering why I was in the team alongside them. They weren't. I know that now but I did have that kind of insecurity when I was given my first chances to play in the Scotland side.

The senior players put up no barriers then and there have never been any barriers as far as I know. Certainly, I've been in the team as a regular for ten years or so now and they have never become apparent to me. When I started off I mixed with the younger players, some of whom played in England. The players from England didn't stick together because they played in England. For instance wee Jimmy Johnstone used to be always with Denis Law and Billy Bremner – and Jimmy was a homebased Scot all through his career. Later as the team changed, my mates in the squads included Joe Jordan and Gordon McQueen, who were both with Leeds, wee Lou Macari, who was then with Manchester United, and Tommy Hutchison who was then with Coventry. Players didn't pick who they hung around with on the basis of whether or not they played in Scotland or in England. They picked them on the only possible basis – whether they got on well with them. It's still the same in the squad now. You're bound to get certain players who stick together but it isn't on the basis of where they play the game.

My view is quite simple. It doesn't matter where you play. If you are Scottish and if you are good enough then you should be picked to play for your country. Which country you play in doesn't enter any of the players' minds. We are all in the thing together and we all pitch in as equals. That's the only way it can be.

Some Scottish club managers have complained about their players being told stories of the fabulous wages they supposedly earn in England. I've read Dundee United's Jim McLean – now Jock Stein's assistant with the Scotland squad – on the subject, and Alex Ferguson of Aberdeen and Jim Clunie who was with St Mirren, have said the same. I can put their minds at rest. In all these years with the Scotland team I've heard the subject of money and wages raised just once and that was when one of the homebased Scots asked a question. When I was being transferred – as I explained earlier – I asked for advice on a personal basis from one of the more experienced players. That was private. Never once did anyone on their own initiative attempt to spell out the wages and the terms which I could have had in England. Anyhow, nowadays most players can find out what the top clubs pay simply by reading the newspapers.

I suppose what really annoys me – apart from the term Anglo itself – are the cries for all-tartan teams which surface periodically. They never seem to be heard when the team is doing well, or even when the team is just about to be picked for an important match. These appeals usually come only when the team has done badly. Then people look for scapegoats, and more often than not it becomes a condemnation of the players who live in England. Why this happens I'll never know. The people who start the witch-hunts are usually also the ones who dwell on the great games of the past. They can rhyme off the Wembley Wizards of 1929, who beat England 5–1 at Wembley. What they don't rhyme off are the teams the players were with – for the simple reason that most of them were just like me and so many others, they earned their living playing in England!

Any successes we have had over the years in which I have been a part of the squad have been achieved by a team which has blended players from clubs on both sides of the border. It hasn't mattered to anyone where the players came from, all that has counted is whether they are the best men for the job. That is the way it should be.

Thank goodness that all-tartan team nonsense hasn't influenced any of the managers I've played under! The idea couldn't work, in any case. If a manager did fall for that rubbish he could have an all-tartan team for one season and then find half the team he had built playing in England the next. Is that any way to build a successful side?

I look on these issues sometimes from a purely personal point of view. I know how I feel about playing for my country. It's something I am very proud to have done and hopefully will continue to do. When I'm injured and out I feel sick. If we've lost I feel terrible. I love playing for Scotland and just because I'm in Liverpool that hasn't changed. Remember too, I can be reporting to the team's HQ in Glasgow just as quickly as, say, the Aberdeen players can travel down from the north-east. Crossing that border doesn't mean that we have moved to the other side of the world.

If we are to be made scapegoats it should be because of how we've played – not because of where we play. Possibly it happens because people back home expect more from us. They might think that we are better players than some of the lads they see every week at home. That isn't necessarily so but they can think that, and they can, at times, look for too much. They might see us on the telly at the weekend and we can look marvellous so they don't expect to see us making any mistakes at all. I've talked about this with Graeme Souness and we came to the same conclusion. When the games are shown on the box all that is seen are the highlights. So people can see you do some great things in the twenty minutes or so of the game. If you have a nightmare spell they don't notice it so obviously. We all have bad games. We all make mistakes, but the artificiality of these match highlights tends to hide that from the general viewing public. They reckon that you are always doing great things, always playing well. That's nonsense. There is no one who *always* plays well. Nightmares can hit the best players in the country and we all know that and live with it. Sometimes, though, the public don't want to believe that and it makes life that little bit harder.

Now I'm getting back to a personal business again – my own form for Scotland. It seems, at times, as if I'm always getting stick. When things are going badly then Dalglish is the player who has to be axed. I've had to live with that for a few years now, had to live with the fact that people still suggest that I never show my club form for my country. It was said when I was with Celtic, and it's been said since I made the move south to Liverpool. Make no mistake, I don't like it. Often it hurts, especially when I reckon that I've done as well as I can in a certain game and yet I'm catching flak for my performance.

I have had bad games for Scotland. But I have also had bad games for Celtic. And bad games for Liverpool. It's not as though I save up these bad days just so I can have them when I'm playing in international matches. Having played eighty games (that's the total as I'm writing this), it's a certainty that some of them have been poor. But in these games I've scored twenty-four goals and remember, for quite a few of the games I've had for Scotland I've been played in the midfield. I've also been picked by four different team managers and two of them, Jock Stein and Willie Ormond, had me as captain of the side on occasions. That doesn't smell too much of failure. After all, I have helped Scotland qualify for three World Cup finals. I don't like to be judged on goals alone. You don't have to be scoring goals to be a success. Other things contribute and Scotland have had success during my time with the team. That is the most important thing because a team always comes before any individual as far as I'm concerned.

Maybe I'm a victim of circumstances just as Denis Law used to be when he was in the team. Denis used to get stick when things went wrong. Now, though, people don't remember any of his bad games. Memory does funny things.

. . .There are occasions when I have to bury my own preferences in playing for the team. When Joe Jordan or Andy Gray are in the side, the team pattern is such that balls are played in high to their strengths. So I have to play a supporting role, getting in to assist Joe or Andy in the penalty box, trying to back up in case they have been able to win the ball and knock it down for me or for someone else. It's a different job from the one I have at Liverpool, but I still take the view that I have to be there as a part of the team. Whether it's being up front trying to help out there, or in midfield if things are going against us, I have to try to adapt my game.

It has been suggested that I suffer personally from taking that attitude. I don't know whether that is the case or not. Frankly, it doesn't matter. I have always seen myself as a part of the team and I'm not going to change in any way now. There would certainly be no chance of me changing just to make myself more popular with the people who criticize me. I prefer to be judged by my fellow professionals. If *they* think that I'm playing badly then that would probably be a more valid judgement than most of the others which have followed me down through the years. Don't get the impression that I'm ducking the issue of my Scotland form. I'm not. I've had to face up to it for a long, long time now and it hasn't got any easier to take.

I admit that I haven't always played well. As I've

explained already, no one can play well all the time. There
have been times, though, when I've felt that I've made a
fair contribution to the game and then found out that I'm
being criticized again. That's when it hurts most. OK, I
can see sometimes that people not involved in the game
might think that a player is contributing less than others.
Yet if they were to go among that player's team-mates,
they could discover that the other players have rated him
highly over the ninety minutes.

It's fair to say that people often see what they want to
see. Like the first time I came back to Hampden to play
after I'd been transferred from Celtic to Liverpool. I
didn't feel any different. I wasn't any different! Yet some
people saw me as being a couple of yards faster. Others
thought I looked fitter than I had ever been before. Still
others thought I seemed more aggressive, only because I'd
moved to England. In the same way, people may say I
don't play well for Scotland because the suggestion has
been made before they've seen me play.

I can remember bad games, but I can also remember
games where I've played as well as I've played with either
of my clubs. I remember the first time I was asked to
captain Scotland, when Willie Ormond was in charge of
the national team for the last time. That was at Hampden
and we destroyed Sweden. We won 3–1 but it could have
been more and I scored one of the goals that night. The
others came from Asa Hartford and Joe Craig who was
then with Celtic.

I remember three victories over England where I felt I'd
played well. I remember scoring goals in two of them: at
Hampden in 1976 when Don Masson and myself scored in
a 2–1 win and then the next year at Wembley when we
won 2–0 and Gordon McQueen and I got the goals.

I remember the two qualifying games against Wales
before the World Cup finals in 1978 – at Hampden when

my shot was deflected by Ian Evans past his own keeper for our win and at Anfield where I scored once and we won 2–0.

I remember the qualifying match against the Czechs for these same finals when we beat them 3–1 at Hampden and I scored again.

I remember scoring the only goal of the game in Tel Aviv which saw us beat Israel on the way to Spain for the 1982 finals.

There are other matches where I have felt that I've played well, just as I've been disappointed in others. The 1974 World Cup finals in West Germany were a disappointment to me personally because I didn't play as well as I should have done. I felt then that I'd let the team down and that's why Spain will be important to me. I hope these finals will be the most memorable of the three Scotland have taken part in since 1974.

It's been a great run for a country which had not qualified since 1958. Now here we are having qualified three times in succession, and I have the chance to play in my third finals when so many players before me didn't even manage to play in one.

That thought can comfort me when I think of the criticism I receive . . .

Qualification, after all, is a huge success in itself. Lots of people underestimate the achievements of Scotland, a nation of only five million people, in qualifying for three successive finals.

I don't, because I am proud to be a Scot, just as Jim Watt and Jackie Stewart who have the same pride.

12
My Scotland mates

Only eighteen months separated the international begin-
nings of myself and my old mate Danny McGrain, who
had kicked off his career at Celtic Park with me. And if
Danny had not picked up the injury which cost him
selection just before we qualified for the World Cup finals
in Argentina, I'm pretty sure that he would have more
international caps for Scotland than I do. If he hadn't
passed my total, then he would definitely be up there
around the same number – and I can't think of anyone
who deserves it more than Danny does. He has contri-
buted so much to any success we have had as an international side, especially at Hampden where his runs forward
have been tremendous. The great thing about Danny is
that when he breaks forward with the ball, he knows what
he is going to do with it. Some defenders burst forward
and then don't have a clue how to finish the move. You
can never say that about Danny. He has come back from
that injury with more aggression in his play, too. I don't
know what's caused that. Maybe it's his age – he's getting
on a bit now (are you reading this, Danny?). Seriously, I
think he has developed this commitment because he
realizes that his career was once almost finished. He was
ill and missed caps and then injury knocked him out of
other games. Now it's difficult for me to name a more
consistent professional.

Danny had his first taste of the World Cup in 1974 and
that's when Jim Holton played too. He was the most
popular player with the punters. He was such an enthu-
siast, big Jim, that this seemed to reach the fans. He was

their hero. He was a great player for Scotland and it was a tragedy when he collected all those injuries one after another, until eventually he dropped out of the picture.

Another player in that World Cup who was a tremendous competitor was Davie Hay. Davie was with me at Celtic then, but he picked up injuries and illness after he was sold to Chelsea and he didn't play for Scotland again after that last match of the finals against Yugoslavia in Frankfurt. That was a terrible blow for Davie, and a blow for the team as well. He was such an important part of the side; no one was able to take on Davie in our midfield. Remember the clash he had with that big Brazilian Luis Pereira in the second game in West Germany. Davie just wasn't afraid of anyone and he had the great knack of getting other players alongside him to show off their skills while he grafted and fought and won the ball. He had a superb World Cup – and then, after that, nothing but trouble. I'm just glad to see that he found success again as a manager with Motherwell and eventually took over as boss at Celtic Park. That World Cup made him, built him a reputation worldwide and then ironically he was never able to play for Scotland again.

Joe Jordan came though in West Germany as well. He has had some outstanding games for Scotland, particularly when he has been facing a Continental side. They fear him in the air. They really do – and when you see him going for a ball can you blame them? I think the Continental teams don't go for high balls as aggressively as British strikers. This gives Joe a vital psychological edge before the match even starts. Defenders don't relish playing against him. He is amazingly courageous and he wins balls that other players wouldn't even get to.

The thing that must cause defenders most worry is knowing that Joe is absolutely fearless. He'll go for a ball knowing that he might get hurt; he doesn't let that stop him. A defender simply doesn't get a minute's rest when he is opposed to Joe. It's never been any surprise to me that foreign coaches often mention Joe's name when they are asked about danger men in the Scottish line-up. He scares most of them to death!

Four years after West Germany the squad had changed a bit. Where we had Billy Bremner in 1974 – I discussed Billy's important role in chapter 5 – in building up to 1978 we had Don Masson as the most influential man in the squad. He wasn't the same type of player as Billy, he didn't have the same drive or aggression, but he was the man who organized most of the on-field ploys for the squad that reached Argentina. It was Don who worked out most of the set pieces, Don who was the playmaker, picking the ball up deep from a position in front of the back four and then starting off most of our attacking moves. He was absolutely vital to the overall team performance. You really couldn't overestimate the role he played in that team. He maybe lacked a bit of pace, but his brain was sharp. He was always trying to be constructive and if he had possessed more pace, perhaps he would have lost a little of the marvellous football intelligence he had. He took free kicks, he took corners, he took penalties, and he was a superb passer of the ball. Because things went wrong in Argentina for everyone, I think Don's contribution in helping us qualify has been overlooked.

Martin Buchan was another good player for Scotland. He always did well. It suited him to be the sweeper in the side, staying at the back tidying things up. His contributions could also be overlooked because Martin made things look easy. He always seemed to give himself plenty of time to clear a ball. He was rarely under pressure and it was reassuring to know he was there at the back. He was another player who liked to build things but when he just had to boot that ball clear he could do it as well as the next one.

Of course the 1978 World Cup brought Alan Rough into the Scotland team and while Roughie has been criticized a lot, especially down in England, he has been a smashing goalkeeper for us. I think he has only lost something like a goal a game in his whole career with Scotland, and in the qualifying games for Spain he let in only two goals in the seven matches he played. How can anyone criticize that record?

It's been said that he might have been an even better goalkeeper if he had been full-time – but I don't know. Playing with Partick Thistle seems to have suited him all these years and the big fellow doesn't perform like a part-timer when he's with Scotland. I'll tell you this, when we qualified for the Argentina World Cup he made a marvellous save from John Toshack at Anfield. And as far as I'm concerned, that save from Tosh counted as much as either of the two goals we got that night in getting us through to the finals. Look too at the campaign which has taken us to Spain. He was solid-looking in Sweden in the opening match of the section; in Israel he had a super game, and when Israel came to Hampden he had two saves one after the other right at the start when the score was still 0–0. They were important saves to make at that stage, when we were still maybe a little nervous, feeling our way a bit in the game. If Israel had scored we would have been under pressure. Instead the saves launched us towards the victory we needed. Again, in Northern Ireland when they put us under pressure towards the end of the game Roughie played magnificently. You won't catch me joining in the chorus of criticism he seems to pick up from the television commentators down south. He did us a right turn in these qualifying games. It was always going to be a tight section and not losing goals helped put us in the driving seat.

In Argentina, John Robertson appeared briefly, but since then he has become a key player in the squad. It's a joy for any player to have Robbo out there on the wing. It doesn't seem to matter how tight the situation is, he seems able to get the ball into the penalty box. He seems to have that little bit extra to whip the ball past defenders and they're not difficult crosses for the likes of us waiting in the box. Usually they are ideal, struck just perfectly to make them easier for us and hard for any defenders. Another thing about Robbo, if he isn't playing well himself – and that isn't too often – he leaves room for others to play. He takes a defender out there wide with him and deep too so that there are gaps for other players to utilize. Frank Gray bursts in there regularly because he and Robbo have an understanding that they developed at club level with Nottingham Forest and brought with them into the Scotland side. If Robbo isn't going to get away from his marker, then he'll make sure that Frank can get past him and hit that by-line if possible. That partnership has worked well for us.

Positioned between these two we have had Asa Hartford, who just missed out on the 1974 World Cup, was with us in Argentina and has re-established himself again under Jock Stein after dropping out for a spell. I've always rated him. He is a tremendous one-touch player, he's difficult to knock off the ball and will work all day. He is always ready to get in and help a team-mate who might be in trouble. Plus he has great vision. I was always surprised that Brian Clough let him go, because he does fit in so well in that little triangle we have on the left, and that could still have been the Forest left side!

My roommate when we're away – with Liverpool and with Scotland – is Graeme Souness. It's been that way since he came to Anfield. Graeme didn't get a chance in Argentina until that last game against Holland in Mendoza. He's been more or less a regular since, and in my book he is the best passer of a ball in Britain. I'm not just talking about the Scottish team now, I'm talking about the whole country. There's no one I would place in front of him for accurate and dangerous passing. He's the best there is. He wins the ball, then distributes it and dictates the pace of the game.

The other Liverpool player in the Scotland team is Alan Hansen, and he could turn out to be one of the top players in the World Cup finals in Spain. Big Alan has superb skills. The way that Scotland have used him has been just right. He has been the sweeper playing alongside Alex McLeish or Willie Miller mainly, and they have been the markers. That's where he is best. It allows him the chance to come forward, and when he does break then the opposition are in trouble. He sees things so well when he is coming from the back. He doesn't appear to be aggressive but he is a competitor. I suppose that is because things have come so easily for him. What I mean is that Alan has natural skills and isn't afraid to use them. The Continentals drool over him and that's why I'm certain he will be outstanding in Spain; the way the game is played at the very top level – and the World Cup is that – will suit him perfectly.

It's been good also to see players from Aberdeen and Dundee United coming into the scheme of things. They have done well with their teams in Scotland, and Jock Stein has given them their chance. Because of the European Cup final I couldn't play in the home internationals in 1981 and so I watched the Wembley game against England on the box. That day Alex McLeish and Willie Miller were magnificent; Davie Narey came on into midfield when wee Asa was taken off injured and he was great as well. Gordon Strachan, of course, has probably been the discovery of this World Cup qualifying series. He

hadn't been in the team until Jock Stein took over and
then there he was playing his first World Cup match ever
in the Solna stadium in Stockholm and sticking away the
goal which brought us that very important win. He was
outstanding that night. In this World Cup though, everyone has had their moments. It might have been Gordon
Strachan in one match, Alan Rough in another, wee
Robbo in another . . . but it's all added up to having a *real*
team effort to get us to the finals this coming summer.
There's a club feel about the international squad. It's
more like it was in 1974 than in 1978, when the team spirit
wasn't nearly as high. Obviously we all want to succeed
but we also want to succeed in the right way. There's more
professionalism about the whole thing and I think that all
the lads have realized that the team's success is much
more important than any individual achievement. Scotland has to come first. That's why we were able to qualify
for Spain at the top of our section. No one in the squad
put themselves ahead of the team effort. Nor do I think
the Big Man (Jock Stein) would have allowed anyone to
do that.

It's all added up to a summer in Spain, when thousands
of Scots will invade the towns where we play and when the
rest of the nation will sit at home praying that the memory
of Argentina will be laid to rest. I hope so too, and I hope
to be in the group of players who go to Spain. I think it
would mean a lot to those of us who were in Argentina to
be able to restore that lost pride. At least partially . . .

13

The road to sunny Spain

It's a strange thing about this game of football, the way in which attitudes can change from one season to the next. Or, in some cases, from one week to the next!

The horrors of Argentina had started to fade from the minds of the fans by the time the draw was made for the qualifying rounds of the 1982 World Cup tournament. That was less than two years after the troubles in Cordoba, and yet the fans once more began to dream of the team reaching the playoffs for the world's greatest soccer prize. 'We're on our way to sunny Spain,' they were singing, even though we had had a far from successful tilt at the European championships in between. Ally MacLeod had gone as manager and Jock Stein, my old boss at Celtic Park, had taken over. He felt that changes had to be made – when he accepted the job our international performances were fairly poor. We had lost our opening game in our European championship group against Austria in Vienna, then we lost to Portugal in Lisbon. It was an unhappy tournament for us. We beat Norway home and away, but we could only draw with Austria at Hampden and we lost home and away to Belgium. We did beat Portugal, soon to be World Cup opponents, at Hampden.

Mind you, while the Belgium defeats were a matter for comment at the time, things didn't look half so bad when they reached the European championship finals in Italy in the summer of 1980. They lost narrowly to West Germany in the final, and the Germans had been the outstanding team in the competition. The Belgians were a hard-working team, a hard-tackling team – I picked up a few bruises which proved that – and had some outstanding individual players like François van der Elst, now at West Ham, who was then with Anderlecht but soon moved on to New York Cosmos.

Anyhow, when the World Cup draw was made, the disappointments of the two years or so immediately before it were swept aside. There we were with Spain beckoning in the distance and four other countries lined up to do battle with us in the group. Drawn with us were Northern Ireland, who were to win the British home international championship in 1980 the year the qualifying games kicked off; Portugal, again, those near neighbours of Spain; Sweden, finalists in 1958 when the tournament was played there and regular competitors in the finals down through the years; and finally Israel, the maverick side pushed into a European section to carry them clear of political troubles in the Middle East, and an obvious unknown quantity as far as the rest of us were concerned.

It was a tough-looking section. We knew from the start that Northern Ireland would be difficult to beat because the knowledge the British teams pick up about each other makes all these games tight nowadays. We were sure that Sweden would be a force because they were a team with a reputation for turning it on whenever the World Cup came around. We felt that the Portuguese would not want to miss out on the affair when the finals kicked off in the country right next door to them. Israel were the worry – I felt from the start that they would give all the countries who played them in Tel Aviv problems. We had one of their players, Avi Cohen, with us at Anfield and while he couldn't get in as a first-team regular he played often enough to prove that he was a class performer. His message to the three Scots at Anfield was simple – 'There are more good players from the same place . . .' We had been warned!

With the change in the number of finalists this time around – twenty-four countries were to be in Spain instead of sixteen, as previously – two countries from the five would go through. It gave us that second chance if necessary, but studying the teams we would have to face still didn't convince me that the business of qualifying was going to be easy. It wasn't.

The manager kept stressing that it was hard work which would get us to Spain. He insisted, 'To qualify you have to wear your working clothes, get on you dungarees. Then when you get to Spain that's the time for the good suits.' He didn't let us get carried away after getting a good result in a game. The way the team responded must have pleased him. Everyone did work hard and that's why we got the results we did. In the end we lost just once, to Portugal in the last game. By then we had qualified, and Portugal were out, so the manager tried one or two experiments in a game which had to be played but which could never count as far as Group Six of the European qualifying zone was concerned.

The way it happened, the results in all of the games we played turned out to be more important than the performances. Lots of times in the past I've seen us play well and get nothing out of games. This time the lads looked on all the games as cup ties. They went out to get the kind of result which would take us to Spain and they succeeded. Maybe we had a break or two, but in a cup competition any team needs that if it is going to be successful. We didn't get any more than our share.

One of the breaks came in that very first game we played in Stockholm. A great shot from one of their players hit the woodwork and bounced back onto Alan Rough, and big Alex McLeish stepped in to boot it away. To balance that, though, we might have had a couple of penalties. There was one glaring offence when Andy Gray was barged down in the box as he was getting ready for a header. Still, these things happen in any game and when Gordon Strachan went through to get that great goal in the second half it was enough for a win. Throughout the game we had as many chances as they did and we took one of them.

It was an important result because we had won away from home to start our campaign, and the victory was against one of the teams that had been rated as possible to go through. With all due respect to Israel, when the section was drawn and even when the games began, they were the team that were being written off. The two places were to be taken from among the other four countries. So, in beating Sweden, we had pushed ourselves immediately clear of one of our main rivals.

Mind you, I wasn't too impressed by the fact that the Swedes had a good World Cup record. That was not going to get them to the finals this time, just as the fact that we had qualified twice in succession wasn't going to do it for us. It was how we performed in the qualifying games and how we found the other teams on the night. I'm not a great believer in tradition carrying teams through. You have to earn anything you get in the game – the past doesn't automatically earn you the right to play, or even to expect to play, in World Cup finals. That has to be won in the qualifying games, which can be very, very tough.

We had begun so well, and then we learned that our very next fixture, the game against Portugal, was to be at Hampden. It was a match which we hoped could push us well clear at the top of the section if we added a home win to the two points we collected in Sweden. It should have gone that way. And it would have done but for one man, Bento, the little goalkeeper from Benfica. A couple of years earlier I'd scored one of four Liverpool goals against him at Anfield. This time it was so different. He still had that eccentric look about him, but at Hampden that night with 60,000 fans watching he had a charmed time. I remember one try I had which I was sure had deceived him. It had in fact, because he dived the wrong way, but the ball came back off his legs. That was the kind of night he had.

When we had played our last European championship game against Portugal at Hampden we had scored four goals too, and we reckoned that Bento would be the weak link. That was less than a year earlier – but the games were vastly different, as I knew they would be. In the first one the Portuguese, like ourselves, were out of the European championships and it seemed a case of going through the motions for them. We were looking for more and we got a good, solid victory, but Bento was not in such good form that night as he was on his return. Nor were the Portuguese as committed in that meaningless game as they were when they returned on World Cup business. They had a new coach, Juca, and a determination they hoped would take them to their first finals since when they finished third in the finals held in England.

Anyhow, we could only draw 0–0. While the result was a disappointment to the fans, the game was still the best we played in all the qualifying matches I was in. Later the home game against Israel matched it, but I missed that one because of injury.

The next game was another trip away from home – and this was a journey into the unknown for most of us. It was the trip to Israel. As well as the warning we had from Avi

Cohen, we had advance notice from the results the Israeli national team had achieved that things were not going to be at all easy for us at the Ramat Gan stadium in Tel Aviv, where the game was played in front of 55,000 fans. In my opinion, that was the hardest game we had to play in the whole group. Israel put us under more pressure than any other team. They also had more shots at goal than any other side in the section. Roughie was our important man in the first half. He did well at a time when they were buzzing. They were well organized and they had been encouraged by draws with Northern Ireland at the same stadium and with Sweden in Stockholm. That had them playing with a lot of fire and they had two front men, Damti and Sinai I think their names were, who had lots of pace and gave us all kinds of trouble.

Things improved for us after half time when Jock Stein changed the team around a little at the back and the defence began to settle. Then, before I took a knock I scored the one goal of the game. We had won a corner on the right and when it came over to the near post it was knocked on to me. I was at the other side of the goal and I just hit it into the net. It was a goal I was pleased about because as well as eventually winning the game, it took a lot of the sting out of the Israeli team. Just after I limped off, Andy Gray, who took over from me, came close to scoring with his first touch of the ball. Eventually the Israeli challenge died away. But, believe me, that opening burst was the worst spell we had in all eight of our qualifying games.

As I say, I had had some worries about that game beforehand, particularly as the games people tell you are the easy ones are always liable to turn out to be the most difficult of all. The most difficult thing when you come to that type of game is your total unfamiliarity with the players you are asked to face. It's always a little easier when you know what to expect: not necessarily just the individual players, but also the general style of play. Going to Sweden to start things off had its problems too, but that wasn't one of them because you knew how they would play. Most of the lads have a lot of European experience and because of that you can generally tell how the Swedes or the Portuguese or any other European country will approach things. When you move out of Europe then your knowledge is necessarily more limited.

The next match was the first against Northern Ireland. I missed it because of injury but it was difficult because the knowledge we have of each other is so detailed. It all comes down to players trying to cancel each other out. When you are playing against most of the team week after week, that increased knowledge becomes as big a problem as knowing nothing at all about a team like Israel. We went a goal behind in that match and then John Wark stepped in to equalize. That was an important goal and Warkie does have a habit of getting goals. Just take a look at his record with Ipswich! I didn't see it so I don't know too much, except what the lads told me later. Obviously it was hard because the Irish played it that way, trying their best not to let us settle. It was, though, in some people's eyes another point lost at Hampden and a disappointment for the 78,444 fans there, but looking positively – as we did – it was another point gained to keep us in control of the section.

Still, the next match at Hampden gave the fans a win and also a few goals to celebrate. The Israelis, under their coach Jack Mansell from England, arrived for the return. They wanted revenge for Tel Aviv and once again they began powerfully. That was when big Roughie saved us right in the opening minutes. Once again I was out because of injury but I saw the saves Roughie made and they were vital for us. After that opening spell, we took control and in the end we won fairly easily 3–1 with John Robertson scoring with two penalty kicks and Davie Provan of Celtic getting the other. Their striker Sinai, who had looked good over there, scored their only goal.

Robbo does take those penalty kicks well. He always looks so perfectly cool when he steps up to take them. I don't suppose he is, because taking penalties in front of huge crowds when so much depends on the outcome isn't something designed to relax you. Yet the wee man takes it all in his stride and simply tucks them away. In the past we made a habit of missing penalties. I remember Billy Bremner having one saved which cost us a victory over West Germany at Hampden shortly before the 1974 finals. We drew 1–1 when we could have notched an important prestige win. Then there was another one against Spain when Tommy Hutchison failed. If he had scored we would have gone on to win that game easily. Instead the miss upset us, inspired the Spaniards and we eventually lost 2–1. That was in a European championship match back in 1974 when we were trying to qualify for the finals. While we did get a draw in Spain the next year, that defeat was the one which stopped us getting through to the late stages of the tournament, something we never have achieved!

The next World Cup game was the following season, right at the start, and it was right where we had kicked off on the road to Spain – back facing the Swedes. This time we had them at Hampden, but suddenly they had been transformed. Older players had been dropped and young-er, fresher players brought in after their dreadful start. As well as losing to us they had dropped a home point to Israel, lost 3–0 to Northern Ireland in Belfast and dropped another point to Israel away from home. At that stage they seemed out of things and everything pointed to a three-way battle between ourselves, Northern Ireland and Portugal. But, as constantly seemed to be happening in that section, things had changed by the time they came to Hampden in September. Two results in the summer had sharpened the Swedes' appetite. They saw the possibility of reaching Spain looming up ahead of them again after two marvellous performances which saw them beat Northern Ireland 1–0 and then the Portuguese 3–0 soon after. So when they came to Glasgow their coach Lars Arnesson was confident once more. He looked at the table and saw his team just two points behind us – though we had a game in hand – and level with Northern Ireland and Portugal, although the men from Lisbon had also played a game less. If he stole a win against us then the Swedes would have leapfrogged to joint top alongside us. As always, Arnesson tried to put pressure on us. He said that his team had little to lose, that Scotland's form at Hampden had not been as impressive as it once had been, that we had been lucky in Stockholm and the same luck for his team would see them through to the finals. After all, he added, this was our last home match and we had to visit Belfast and Lisbon.

In a sense he was right. His team did have a really good chance of qualifying once again. But that only underlined to us that this was a game where we would have to be at our very best. We knew what we had to do. We had to win and by doing that we would end Sweden's hopes; qualification would be beyond them and we would have reached ten points. That was our target, a total which Jock Stein had always maintained would be enough to take any team from the section to Spain. It would not be enough to clinch the qualification, but it would keep us out in front and the others would have to go some to catch us.

The fans could scent Spain. They could see the sunshine already and they turned out as they always do at Hampden to give us the kind of backing other countries envy. The banners and the flags were waving as we came out and, while we didn't have to be told how important the game was, the roar which greeted us did let us know how these fans felt. To them this was the crunch. A win over the Swedes, as far as they were concerned, would put us in an unassailable position.

Over 81,000 fans were there that night – an astonishing attendance when you consider that the Swedes are not the most fashionable of opponents. As the competition had gone on, so the attendances had risen. Portugal had started the Hampden games with just 60,000, then came Northern Ireland with 78,444; the unknown Israelis drew an amazing 61,489 and finally the Swedes packed in 81,511. It meant that the four home World Cup games had drawn more than 280,000 fans, and proved again just how much the competition that Scotland once spurned now means to the supporters.

It's hard for us to believe today that back in 1950 we turned down the chance of playing in the World Cup finals in Rio. Then you could take part by invitation and we were asked, but decided we would only go if we won the British championship. We didn't because England beat us at Hampden 1–0. They went to Brazil where they lost to the United States in one of the biggest shocks the tournament has ever seen; we stayed at home on the sidelines for another four years.

Back to that Swedish game. When we took the lead through Joe Jordan after just twenty-one minutes the game was only going one way. They had come set to rely on defence, try to lure us out and then hit us on the break. But we sensed that and so we were cautious all the while we were looking for goals. Our second goal – we won 2–0 – came ten minutes from the end when Andy Gray was brought down in the penalty box and little Robbo tucked away another penalty. The Swedes didn't really trouble us and although I was substituted in the second half I felt that it had been one of my best games for Scotland. Again it was a team effort, and that's how it was in the last game that mattered in the section – in Belfast against Northern Ireland.

It wasn't the best of trips for us because of the troubles in that city. I suppose you always go there thinking that a team could become a target for terrorists, and being surrounded by security men even when you are sitting down to meals in your heavily guarded hotel doesn't put you in the mood for a game.

We'd only played there once before since the troubles started, mainly because the Scottish Football Association had always feared that the fixture could throw up problems for us because of the clear historical links between the Scots and the Northern Irish. Since 1970 – before my time – the Northern Irish had played all their games at Hampden. Then in 1980 we went to Belfast for a British championship game which we lost 1–0, and the Irish went on to win the British international championship for that season. They deserved it too, and we all knew that this second trip across the Irish Sea was not going to be a joyride. The Irish needed a win to maintain their challenge while we needed just one single point to make sure of going to Spain. By that time, we knew that eleven points would take us to the finals.

We knew that a draw would be enough, but there was no way that Jock Stein sent us out to defend. Sure, he sent us out to make things as difficult as possible for them. It was up to us to frustrate them and let them chase after a goal while we could afford to sit back, much the way a team playing a European Cup game can do when away from home in a first leg. It had to be a patient kind of game, a disciplined performance quite unlike so many of those in the past when we have gone off upfield chasing goals instead of making sure that the result we want is achieved. I've been in teams when that has happened and all it has led to is some kind of glorious failure. We wanted a draw, or if we could get it, a win. Despite all their pressure we made as many goal chances as they did over the ninety minutes.

They tried all the time to turn it into an old-fashioned British cup tie. They had their two big fellows up front, Billy Hamilton and Gerry Armstrong, and Pat Jennings was hitting long balls upfield towards them, hoping they could win them and put our back men under pressure. We were without Alex McLeish, who was injured, but Alan Hansen and Willie Miller coped with them well – Alan was the best player on the park. Roughie had one good save from Hamilton near the end and Asa Hartford cleared one shot off the line, but though they created a lot of pressure around our box towards the end of the game, we got the point we needed.

The Irish lads were sick and I felt sorry for them. A few hours later as we were flying back to Glasgow the shock news came through from Lisbon that Portugal had lost at home to Sweden. Suddenly the Irish were back in contention in a section which had been cut-throat all the way. That was the last result anyone expected, and it proved again that if the Swedes had taken anything at all from us at Hampden they could have been on the doorway to Spain themselves.

Eventually Portugal lost to Israel away from home and by the time we went there to play our last game it was

meaningless. They couldn't qualify, we had already qualified, and the drama was to take place in Belfast. The Irish
duly won against Israel 1–0 and they were through to
Spain along with us. It's exactly what we would have
asked for in the beginning. To get two British teams
through from the same section was a great bonus and it
was nice for us too that our Lisbon match was not going to
decide the Irish fate. They had that in their own hands
after the collapse of Portugal.

I am glad that Northern Ireland got through because for
at least two of their players, Pat Jennings and Chris
Nicholl, it will be their last chance of playing in a World
Cup finals. It would have been a tragedy for Pat, in
particular, if he had gone through as tremendous a career
as his and missed out on the finals in Spain. It was great
for all of them – Billy Bingham, their manager and a
neighbour of mine in Southport, has a very good squad of
players – but it was just extra nice that the two veterans
got there.

The Irish seem to have a great team spirit, possibly
helped by the fact that they have a small squad of players.
Billy Bingham isn't able to make too many changes
because he knows that the talent available is not nearly as
plentiful as in other countries. Because of that, the squad
seem to have become closely knit and they have the same
sort of club feeling that I can sense in our own squad this
time.

The strange thing about that World Cup qualifying
section if you look at the cold statistics is that we did worst
of all against Portugal. We won just one point against
them. That came at Hampden in our 0–0 draw, though
they were lucky to survive against us that night. Very few
fans turned out to watch in Portugal because they knew
that the Portuguese had failed to reach the finals, and we

couldn't get too excited because we had done the job and qualified before getting to the Stadium of Light.

Our boss took the chance to try out one or two players like Paul Sturrock up front; Alan Rough had been injured in training and Billy Thomson was in goal. It wasn't the changes, though, that brought us our only defeat in the section – it was the atmosphere. Or rather, the lack of atmosphere. I would like to play that game over again with a full stadium. It would have helped us, I think, more than them. The lack of atmosphere made for a slow game and that suited them down to the ground. They like to play it slow but we need more pace and more aggression than you saw in that match. A big crowd would have helped produce that. I'm not suggesting that we revert to our old ways, that we play like the Irish played against us for instance, trying to do everything at 100 miles an hour. There is somewhere in between the two extremes which suits us, where we can push the ball about patiently but lift the pace of the game when we feel that is needed. We never were able to in Lisbon.

I don't go all the way with the Boss changing the team around a bit for that match. I'm not saying that because I started off on the bench – it would have been nice to go through the section unbeaten. It was probably right to leave John Robertson out because he had picked up a caution earlier and another would have had him banned from the first match in the finals. There was no point in risking that. Dropping him allowed Paul Sturrock of Dundee United to come in away from home and score a goal which must give him confidence for the future. He was playing for Dundee United when I was with Celtic but he has been improving steadily in the years I've been away. It was the first time I'd seen him for a while, although I'd caught snatches of him on the box when

Dundee United were playing UEFA Cup games. He had looked good in these – sharp and quick and able to give defenders trouble even when he is left upfield on his own. He displayed these talents in Lisbon, and he took his goal superbly before we went down 2–1.

It was, despite the hiccup in Lisbon, a very successful campaign. We had done particularly well away from home, whereas in the past we had always relied on our Hampden form to take us through. The really important results had turned out to be the ones in Sweden and in Israel. Beforehand we would have settled for three points out of four against both these countries. Instead we took all four each time and the extra ones were bonus points. First because we didn't expect to pick up full points from the matches and, second, because no other country was able to win in either place. Nowadays it doesn't matter in international football who you are playing against, if you win away from home it's an achievement. Basically there are no easy games at international level. The smaller countries, those once written off as weaker, are so much better organized these days. Even at club level we find it harder and harder to get good results away from home in places like Finland or Iceland. Just watch any of the results and you will see that.

I feel sorry that Wales didn't qualify after leading their section and making all the running in it for so long. Yet they failed against little Iceland. And that match was at home! Their manager Mike England decided on an attacking formation to try to get goals in case their group would be decided on goal difference. He altered the team's normal style of play and they could only draw 2–2. It was a gamble that failed and it was the kind of thing that has happened to Scotland before.

I don't think that Jock Stein would ever make that kind

of mistake! The Big Man took over the team when things had been going badly, just a few months after Argentina, and it was obvious that someone with standing was required to lift the morale of the whole country. No one in the game in Scotland has earned greater stature than Jock Stein and he is the biggest benefit of all to the side as we prepare for Spain. He is an awesome personality and it's hard sometimes not to be completely inhibited by his presence. It's possibly important for some of the players not to be too overawed by him. Everyone has respect for him and for his achievements, and I think it eases pressure on the players when they believe in someone who is in command. He may not have been over the World Cup course before, but there's only one or two managers who can match his European experience; the knowledge he has picked up down through the years since he won the European Cup with Celtic in 1967 will help us all in Spain. Other managers know of his reputation too and they will be apprehensive about crossing swords with him. Foreign journalists and TV or radio men concentrate on him and he handles them superbly, which stops too many of us having to get involved with that side of things when all we really want to do is prepare for and play in the games. Little things like that can become very important when the pressures begin to build during the World Cup finals themselves. The Big Man helps to shield us from the publicity machine which goes into action on these occasions.

Big Jock has always taken a positive view in the games so far; he has been much more concerned with what we do ourselves than with what the opposition are going to do. He has concentrated on that, although obviously he has been able to fill us in on certain aspects of the other team's play. Even in Belfast, he told us that we weren't going out there to defend. We weren't going out there to play for a draw, but if we got a draw then we could be content with that.

The other thing is that there is no way that big Jock will make promises about what we are going to do. He won't be setting outrageous targets. He'll be happy if we go to Spain, play well and do better than we've done before. So far, in all the appearances we have made, no Scottish team has been able to get past the opening section games. We'll also be properly prepared in that we will know about the opposition. The manager will be there to watch them before we play in the games. I'm not suggesting that he'll hand out dossiers to the players, but he will be able to point out possible danger men. Again, he'll stress where our own strengths will lie for each match. It will be a new experience for him, even with all the years he has been at the top. For the spell that you are there, you feel constantly under the spotlight. But I'm convinced that he can handle all of that after close on twenty years of involvement in top-level European football. And he's shown already that in no way will anyone be allowed to get carried away on a World Cup bandwagon. It's only right that we should enjoy our success, savour the fact that we have qualified for the World Cup for the third time in succession. Because, after all, that is something to be proud of. But no one will become too involved in the euphoria which is bound to get underway among the fans as they begin to pack their suntan oil and book their trips to Spain this summer.

Jock Stein has proved himself over and over again as a club manager, but I think that perhaps he will want to prove himself as a Scotland manager too. To do that he will want the disciplined on-field performances which were a key to our successful qualifying run. He insisted on that discipline and he will want to see it maintained. If we do it, then perhaps we can do better than any team which has gone before us, and Jock Stein will be the most successful manager Scotland has ever had.

Editor's Note

In the end the Scots failed to qualify – once again failing to get through the first stages on goal difference. And it was an unhappy World Cup series for Kenny Dalglish himself. He played in the opening game against New Zealand and scored one of the Scots' five goals. The others came from John Wark (2), John Robertson and Steve Archibald.

But, following that match in Malaga, Dalglish was relegated to the bench for the second-section game in Seville against the Brazilians. He did make an appearance to replace Gordon Strachan in the second half as the searing heat took its toll on the Scots and they slumped to a 4–1 defeat.

Then he was dropped completely by manager Jock Stein for the deciding match against the Russians. The Scots drew that one in Malaga 2–2 but goal difference edged them out as Dalglish watched from the stand surrounded by his adoring Tartan army.

Once again there were those who wrote him off and once again his own astonishing resilience surfaced to bring him back into the Scotland side. The following season he returned to play one of his greatest games for his country against European champions Belgium in the Heysel stadium in Brussels. He scored both the Scots' goals in a narrow 3–2 defeat and clearly re-established himself as a key player in the Scotland setup. So much so that Graeme Souness, his Liverpool and Scotland team-mate for so long, now with Sapridoria, confidently predicts that Dalglish will be an important figure in an amazing *fourth* World Cup campaign.

Only injuries and club calls prevented him reaching the 100 caps total by the summer of 1984. Knowing the man, who would bet against him reaching it to thrust himself well clear of his nearest challenger as Scotland's most capped international player!

14

Maybe the hardest – not necessarily the best!

The English First Division is supposed to be the best in the world. I've got two championship medals at home so it would be nice to think so, but I'm not convinced about these claims.

It could be the hardest to win, though I've doubts about that which I'll elaborate on in a moment. But where I differ with lots of people is when they confuse *hardest* with *best*. Because the two don't necessarily go together. Its great competitiveness doesn't make it better than any other league in the world. As far as I'm concerned you would need to have studied other leagues, or even played in them, before you started making these extravagant claims. Otherwise I think it's impossible to say one is better than another.

Now, don't go getting me wrong on this. I'm not knocking the league where I earn my living, but I don't want simply to pay lip service to claims that I don't agree with.

You see, I have experienced playing in another league. I played in Scotland with Celtic in both the old-style First Division and in the Premier League, so I can talk about these two competitions. They say it's harder to win the English title than the Scottish one, but I'm not ready to accept that. Probably because Celtic was the club everyone went gunning for. Which is exactly the way I find it down here with Liverpool. The same kind of pressure applied to both clubs. Every time Celtic played it was like a cup tie, which made it extra difficult to win the title for

Celtic. OK, maybe some of the teams down near the foot of the table weren't as good as teams here in England. Yet when they faced Celtic their commitment was total. Having that kind of attitude against you week after week made it very difficult to win the Scottish title. It was as hard for Celtic to win the league as it is for Liverpool to win it down here.

Liverpool also have to cope with other teams lifting their game against them. It's a constant battle, though, when people are expecting you to be at the top, to stay successful all the time. Winning the title is just as hard in either of the countries, and I should know because I've done it on both sides of the border. I'll allow that the English First Division has more strength in depth. I wouldn't argue about that. All I'm talking about is the actual winning of the championship.

Naturally I've been delighted to win the championship medals with Liverpool because the English League is the *toughest* test of a team over as season. My only disappointment to date is that I haven't been able to help the team to win the English Cup; that's the one prize missing from my years in the game, and it's the one I'd like to add to my collection of medals before my career is over. But if I don't win any more, I will still have been successful and happy with the club.

I moved to Liverpool to try to make myself a better player – others will have to judge whether I succeeded or not – and also to win as many honours as possible, particularly in Europe. Well, I have two European Cup medals, two League championship medals and a League Cup medal to add to all the prizes I had already won in Scotland. So the decision was the right one for me to make, and I've loved every minute of my time at Anfield.

It has been hard. Playing up front for the club is tough.

When you are up there you just have to accept that you are going to take punishment. Basically you have to realize that you are going to be kicked by defenders, and there isn't a whole lot you can do about it. I don't like it – who would? – but it's part of the game. I know that I'm going to be kicked in every game I play, and while it's good to get some protection now and again from referees it isn't always there.

I'm not talking about favours from referees when I use the word protection. It's fairly simple, or should be. Either you are allowed to tackle from behind or you are not. If the referee says before the game he is going to allow that then fair enough, he's the gaffer. If, on the other hand, he warns players before the game that there must be no tackling from behind and then after the game has gone ten minutes he is letting these tackles go, I think forwards have reason to feel annoyed. That happens, by the way. The referees and the FA tried to clean the game up a few years ago and it worked OK for a spell. Now though, these tackles are creeping back into the game. Obviously in the position I play, I'm a prime target, but as long as someone isn't diving in trying to break my leg I'll take it and get on with the game. It's the only way to be. You have to learn to take punishing tackles when you are asked to play in or around the opposition penalty box.

We have lots of hard games every season, every game is a cup tie, but West Ham have impressed me every time we have been up against them. And Southampton are a very formidable home team. Other than that we have the Merseyside derby games which set the whole city alight. My time with Celtic helped get me ready for them: the rivalry at the Old Firm clashes with Rangers is even more intense than it is down here basically because of the religious aspects.

People always ask me which players impress me, but honestly I don't have too many favourites outside the teams I have played for. All are in red jerseys or in the dark blue of Scotland or the green and white of Celtic. Usually I am too involved in my own game to take too much notice of other players. Mind you, I was pleased for the English lads at Anfield when England finally qualified for the World Cup. They had been under a bit of pressure. Anfield will have quite a contingent in Spain if all goes well for us between now and then. Hopefully I'll be there with Graeme Souness and Alan Hansen, while Phil Neal, Phil Thompson and Terry McDermott could be there with England. We don't actually talk about the international scene too often in the dressing room, although a fair bit of stick is thrown about from time to time. Like when England lost in Norway and looked as if they might fail to qualify. Graeme came in on the Friday morning just after the England team had got back from Oslo, with a tape of 'Viva Espana' blaring out from his cassette recorder!

The English lads took that all right, because they have given us a bit of the same at times. Really, though, it was good that they reached Spain because they did have to take a lot of criticism, and not all of it was fair. I remember the Saturday they lost away to Switzerland. According to the panel on the telly, everything was wrong with the game in England. Right through from the grass roots, it was all wrong. Directors got it. Coaches got it. Players got it. Even the fans got it because they had caused trouble that night in Switzerland. Everything, but everything, was wrong. Even rules had to be changed if it could bring an improvement to the game. That was one Saturday. The next Saturday – just one week later – England beat Hungary 3–1 in the Nep stadium in Budapest and there was not a mention of all these sweeping reforms. England were back in again with a chance of qualifying. I'm just waiting to see how many changes will happen. It'll surprise me if there are any.

I didn't expect to see the British international championship being so dramatically changed – but I always knew that the game against England would survive. I couldn't understand England trying to have the game at Hampden put off before leaving for Spain.

There was no way I could understand Ron Greenwood's reasoning for wanting to do without the game. Perhaps he was afraid of injuries at that late stage, which is natural. That match is always tremendously competitive! But, that aside, I think it is a good game to have before we head off for Spain. If you have friendly matches then all the players know that they are friendlies. You can call them prestige games if you like, but the lads know that there is nothing at stake. There is no way that you ever get players taking it easy in the Scotland–England game and this is the hundredth game between the two nations, which also makes it special. Remember, the English take the match as seriously as we do. I've certainly noticed that since I moved to Liverpool. They might try to pretend that they don't, but they want to defeat us just as much as we want a win over them. The only difference is that they don't make as much noise about it – neither the players nor the supporters! Personally it's a game I'd welcome before going to Spain, because when we get there we are going to feel pressure, so we might as well get used to it at Hampden a couple of weeks earlier.

There is no substitute for matches and that's why I see the England game as part of the buildup, and a valuable part. Jock Stein has arranged other games too. We'll be together for matches in February against Spain, in March against Holland, in April against Wales and then in May against Northern Ireland and England. In these games performances will be more important than results. After that Jock Stein has booked the squad into a hotel on the Algarve in Portugal, where we will spend a week before heading across the border into Spain. That week is vital too, because players in this country play so many more games than those in any of the other countries involved in the finals that we will need some rest before the matches kick off. In Portugal the squad will train of course, but they'll be able to relax a little too and that could be as important.

The season is long and hard in Britain, and when we get to the World Cup finals we will have played more games and spent less time together than other squads. Many teams will have been together for months thinking about nothing else. We will have been playing probably two games a week right up until the end of the season. That's life in British football – but I'd never dream of going anywhere else. It might not be the best, but it suits me.

15
A beating from the Brazilians

The match against Flamengo of Brazil in Tokyo in the World Club championship was never a game which excited me – not before we embarked on that trip across the world . . . and certainly not after the 3–0 beating we took from the Brazilians in the Olympic stadium in the Japanese capital. The World Club championship had always seemed an artificial competition to me, not something which could compare with the European Cup, for example. That it was to take place in Tokyo, that sponsorship had been guaranteed, merely emphasized what I felt. I had thought the same a year earlier when Nottingham Forest jetted off to play in the game, the first time a British team had taken part since the troubles experienced by Celtic and Manchester United against Argentinian teams in the sixties.

After those, and stories of trouble on the field when Feyenoord of Holland and Bayern Munich of West Germany took part in the contest, we had not subsequently accepted the invitations that followed our wins in the European Cup. Then, after taking the trophy in Paris for the third time and encouraged by Forest's experience the year before, the club decided that we should compete for the trophy for the first time. Again the game was to be staged in Japan and Flamengo of Brazil were to be our opponents.

When it was announced that we were going, I felt a little saddened. Don't get me wrong, I'm not trying to have a go at the club. It's just that as far as I'm concerned – and I'm sure a lot of people in the game feel the same way – the match for the World Club championship doesn't have any great standing. You could walk on to the Kop any Saturday afternoon and ask the fans there who the previous winners have been. They won't be able to tell you. They don't know and they are not terribly interested. I think that the fans realize the truth that the game is staged primarily as a commercial venture. The fact that it is taking place in Japan, so far away from either Europe or South America, helps to underline my point.

This is not sour grapes because we lost the game, either. I held this view from the beginning, and if the economics of the game in this country were as strong as they were a few years back, then I'm almost certain that we would not have gone to play Flamengo at all. But there is a recession, gates have been down, and the club stood to earn a lot of money from playing the one game. The stadium was a sellout, Toyota sponsored the match, and more than forty countries took the game on television. Yet in spite of that interest, I still see it solely as a money-making exercise. If it came round again, I, like everyone else at the club, would play in it if the board and the gaffer decided we should. But it would be more important to me that we'd qualified for it by winning the European Cup than it would be to take that world title.

We helped make them look good by not challenging as powerfully as we might normally have done, but the result of the game could so easily have been closer. Take their goals. The first one, in thirteen minutes, came from a pass by Zico over Phil Thompson's head for Nunes to score. Phil blames himself for that one. The second goal, twenty minutes later, came after a free kick from Zico which Bruce Grobbelaar our keeper stopped but couldn't hold. Adilio reached it to put that one in the net. Bruce blamed himself for not keeping the ball in his hands. The third goal was again scored by Nunes and again from a Zico pass. It looked well offside.

We did manage to make a few chances for ourselves. Craig Johnson clipped one just past, Terry Mac saw a shot touched over by the goalkeeper, David Johnson saw a try blocked, and Ray Kennedy had one stopped by the keeper. We could have had a goal or two even though we didn't play well; when we had missed one of these chances they ran upfield to score themselves. You don't get any breaks when you're playing badly, do you? It's true that you have to earn them.

For that reason it would be nice to have another crack at the world title, just to show people how much better we can play. How it could be done, I don't know. None of us enjoyed the trip to Japan, though I suppose we might have to make that marathon trip once more if we were able to win the European Cup for a fourth time. It's the only way to have the game – if it is necessary to play it at all – in a one-off situation. I wouldn't like to play in a two-legged tie. For one thing we have too many games already. Second, the troubles of the previous two-legged matches would surely haunt the fixture if it was revived in that form.

When I say that we didn't enjoy the Tokyo trip, I don't mean our stay in the Japanese capital. It was the flight. The journey from Liverpool takes more than a day, and the jet lag has you waking in the middle of the night for the first two or three days. The people themselves were amazingly polite and helpful. They were obviously honoured to stage the game, and while the atmosphere is different from Anfield they enjoyed the contest. They don't cheer the way the fans do at home, just applaud when something happens that they like or produce a long-drawn-out shout if the goalkeeper kicks a long ball. Bruce had a few of these with his kicks from hand. They liked watching that.

I just wish that we had given them something more to applaud in our performance, something they would have remembered. That way the trip would have been a whole lot more worthwhile than it turned out.

16

The future dilemma

The eternal dilemma for every footballer comes at the end of his career. That's when he has to decide exactly what he's going to do for the rest of his life.

Like everyone else I'm going to have to face up to that question within the next few years. Right now I just don't know what I will do. Straightaway the idea of football management comes into mind, or coaching, or something within the game, because after all so many players are like myself and have known virtually nothing else. I had a wee while shovelling up wood chips and shavings when I was an apprentice joiner, but that is hardly training for a future which is stretching out ahead of me a whole lot longer than my football career has been.

I've thought about staying in the game, like every player does I suppose. And I've wondered just what it would be like to have a life outside of football. Some people can adapt to that quite easily, others find themselves drawn back to the game because they have missed it so badly. Take Billy McNeill, who was captain of Celtic for so many years. I can remember Billy telling me time and again that he would get out of football when he finished playing. He had business interests while he was a player and he was going to concentrate on them. He was adamant that he wouldn't be a manager. Where is he now? He's manager of Manchester City after spells with Clyde first of all, then Aberdeen and Celtic. The call of the game was too powerful to resist when he was given an opportunity to take over a club.

Billy had a big plus on his side, of course. He was always very articulate and he was able to get his point over to people, so I'm sure he is able to communicate as a manager too. I wonder sometimes if I might have problems that way. But then you never do know until you try it.

Other players have started at the bottom and I admire them. Perhaps that's where you can really learn the job. As long as the club was being run on the right lines, that the people in charge and the players had ambition, then it would be interesting. It wouldn't concern me that everything was going to be so different from Liverpool. I know what problems these smaller clubs have. In my career I've been lucky because I've been with the big teams, with Celtic and with Liverpool. But I realize that's just one side of things. We have a lot of luxuries at Liverpool and you get used to staying in good hotels and having top-class meals and travel. Maybe some of the lads take that for granted. I don't. I'm still grateful that I've been lucky enough to play the game at the top level. If I had to go to a smaller club, though, I'd cut my cloth to suit what it could afford.

I have tremendous admiration for so many of the players I've played with or against who have taken over small clubs. There's Billy Bremner making a go of things at Doncaster Rovers; Alan Clarke first and then Norman Hunter, revitalizing Barnsley; of my old Liverpool mates, Emlyn Hughes who was with Rotherham and, above all, John Toshack who did so much for Swansea.

Tosh worked miracles for quite a spell at the Vetch Field and I must admit that watching that happen makes the job seem attractive. It's encouraging. Yet I know that for all the people I have mentioned there are so many others who have failed and been given the sack. It's a hard way to earn a living.

If the chance doesn't come then I'd have to look around

for some kind of business opportunity. I don't know what it would be, but it's important to me that I get something behind me when I finish playing, something which will assure the future for my family. My parents and my wife Marina's parents did everything possible to make sure that we had a better life than they had had. We did, too, I know that. So it's up to me to try to provide a still better life for my own children. That will be uppermost in my mind when it comes to making any decision about my future.

At the moment I have an interest in a pub, a family affair which is run by Marina's dad, Pat Harkins, back in Glasgow. It's a pub called Dalglish's and it's in Shettleston Road in Glasgow and I make sure that I'm in there to see the regulars whenever I'm up in Glasgow. It helps keep me in touch with my native city. As regularly as possible a bus comes down from the pub to watch our games at Anfield which I really appreciate. It makes me feel good to know that Glasgow people are travelling 200-odd miles to come and support me, because while I may not necessarily ever go back there to live, I'm a Glasgow boy born and bred. I'd never want to change that.